The Recent Graduate's Guide to Job Hunting

How to Move from Backpack to Briefcase

By John Franklin

About the Author:

John Franklin is a communications instructor with the National Foreign Affairs Training Center in Arlington, Virginia.

ISBN-13: 979-8645388478

Also available as e-book through Amazon Kindle.

The Recent Graduate's Guide to Job Hunting

How to Move from Backpack to Briefcase

By John Franklin

For Linda, who lived every lesson herein with me.

The Recent Graduate's Guide to Job Hunting

Table of Contents

WELCOME TO REALITY 101

*"I did not begin to write novels until I forgot
all I had learned in school and college."*

- *John Galsworthy*

Congratulations, graduate. After twelve years of required schooling and four years of accredited higher education, you're now finally ready to step out on your own and make your way in the world.

Undoubtedly, the dean's speech probably went on a bit too long, and maybe too many of your parents' friends peppered you with useless advice that you had to politely pretend to accept, but now that you're done and finally here, one thought undoubtedly races through your mind:

Now what do I do?

If you're like most new grads, you probably have a degree in something you found interesting and thought about making into a career. Maybe you're among those fortunate few who know what they want and are on their way to grad school, law school, or medical school with dreams of legal practice, medicine or some similar future ahead of you.

If not, or if you're among that other majority of recent graduates who have arrived at this point with no real clue how to get wherever you are going (wherever that may be) or who need some time to figure out the working world a bit before heading off to graduate school, *relax*. This is only the beginning.

A few things to note before we begin, however. This book is intended as a step-by-step preparation guide for helping you with your job search, interview preparation, and the inevitable follow-up processes associated with getting a head-start on your career. It is not intended as a means for determining what you want to do in life. Simply put, no guide book or counselor make that determination. What's more, even if you *think* you know what you want to do, chances are that will change over time. According to a variety of sources, the average graduate today can expect to have between four and six careers – not jobs, *careers* – *in* his or her lifetime (and this is quite probably on the low side). In fact, history is full of people who started down one path only to wind up in another. Consider:

- Michael Crichton, author of *Jurassic Park* and numerous other techno-thrillers started out as a medical student.

- John Grisham, author of *The Firm* and other legal masterpieces, began – not too surprisingly – as a lawyer.

- Harry Truman, 33rd president of the United States, was originally a farmer and – wait for it – a haberdasher.

- Carly Fiorina, the first female CEO of Hewlett-Packard, had no idea what she wanted to do with her life when she graduated from Stanford in 1976 with a degree in *medieval studies*.

- Steve Jobs, the man who went on to found Apple and help jump-start the personal computer revolution and the iPod and iPhone, said that one of his original interests had been typefaces and calligraphy before he drifted into computers – this was why Apple's machines had been the first to have multiple typefaces that made them so visually stunning.

The point is, no matter what you may be thinking you'll do with your life, chances are it will change several times over the next twenty or thirty (or even forty or fifty) years. What *won't* change, however, is the importance of knowing how to position yourself, how to get ahead of your competition, and how to impress and win over potential employers. Most people learn this one way or another through the school of hard knocks, but armed with some tips and strategies that you'll find here, you may just get a bit of a break when looking to land that first job.

The Ugly Truth

Before we dive into the strategies, and few preliminaries are in order – and prepare yourself, because not all are going to be pleasant.

First, *the door has slammed shut on college and your extended childhood.* This means that from this point forward, you are going to be judged according to a whole new world of professional standards and expectations, few of which will be fair. If you really want to stand out from your peers, you're going to need to leave as little as possible to chance. More specifically, it means the following:

- **Cutting your hair if you're a guy.** Leave the ponytails and dreads for the service sector. If you walk into someone's office and find yourself competing against a cleaner-cut version of yourself with a professional outlook and attire, you'll already have put yourself at a disadvantage before even getting up to bat. It is admittedly unfair that the hiring manager in front of you probably sported long hair and a tie-dye t-shirt in his college days (or a lip and eyebrow piercing in hers), but sporting anything but a clean-cut image in a first interview is more likely than not a good way to begin things on the wrong foot and spend the majority of the rest of your time playing catch-up.

- **Covering the tattoos and removing the excess jewelry**. Again, an office is always interested in projecting a professional appearance, and this means doing as little as possible that will disturb or offend potential customers. You and your friends may have tasteful body art and consider people with hang-ups over them to be holdovers from your parents' generation, but again, *you don't want to leave anything to chance* when it comes to having your shot at landing a position. Even waiters and waitresses at reasonably priced restaurants are known to cover wrist tattoos with bracelets or wear scarves to conceal neck and shoulder art. It's never a mistake to err on the side of caution in order to minimize any likely issues.

- **Dressing the part.** A job interview – like the job itself – is admittedly an exercise in what could best be described as "professional theatre." In other words, it's about playing a part. Just as you might behave differently in front of parents or grandparents and teachers, so you'll be expected to tone things down when you're in an office setting. (Why do you think people go so crazy at five o'clock on Fridays? It's because in addition to having the weekend to look forward to, they can finally *relax* and be themselves.) This means – again – erring on the side of caution when it comes to your clothes. This doesn't mean having to dress like you're going to a formal event, but play it safe. Ditch the frayed jeans, denim miniskirts, and sneakers and spend some of the graduation money (assuming you have any left) on a few pairs of decent business casual clothes.

Admittedly, this is an unpleasant transition and not one that many people fresh out of school are necessarily eager to make. (And yes, you can certainly expect some hazing from your friends who are still in school about how you've sold out and gone corporate.) But again, when in doubt, ask yourself *what will give me an advantage over someone else walking into this office for a job*? When you get right down to it, that question alone will probably give you more guidance than any suggestion or instructional book ever will.

A Word on Internships

If you were among the smarter and more prescient students and managed to land an internship during your college years, give yourself a well-deserved pat on the back. Not only will this look great on your resume, but it will also provide you with something else that will go a long way toward helping you get started: references.

If, however, you're like a lot of people and spent your summers waiting tables or helping out at your mom's office or dad's business – or living it up on the beach someplace - your start is admittedly going to be a bit more difficult. You're going to have to make some connections now without the benefit of having any under your belt already, and that means having to try a little bit harder. A few people you might consider reaching out to for references:

- **Teachers and professors** – If you had a college instructor you liked or a high school teacher who wrote you a letter of recommendation that you've kept in touch with, don't be shy about reaching out again to see if that person would mind being a reference for you. The worst that is likely to happen is that they will not respond as opposed to declining outright (unless they have reason not to want to recommend you, in which case you have an entirely different issue to address). Don't be afraid to ask them to speak to your *dedication, hard work, attention to detail, perseverance,* *preparation*, and even your *writing and speaking skills*. All of these will come in handy at crunch time.

- **Old bosses from part time jobs**. You say you spent all your summers doing nothing but flipping burgers or lifeguarding at the community pool? Don't worry, chances are people there would be happy to put in a good word on your behalf. If you made any effort to stay in touch or got to know people during the summer, reach out to reconnect.

- **Former coworkers**. Sure, these might be unpaid interns like yourself who spent most of their time playing computer games in an unoccupied cubicle over the summer or trying to make bets over who could drink the most coffee before going to the restroom, but to a prospective employer, they are *coworkers* who can speak to your skills, professionalism, and work ethic (though you may admittedly want them to forego the coffee contest part).

- **Mom and dad's friends**. Admittedly, reaching out to the 'rents at this point in your life is something you probably would rather avoid, but just remember, *it doesn't hurt.* If your dad has a golf buddy who's known you since high school or your mom has a friend who tutored you in geometry when you were struggling to learn the Pythagorean theorem, these are people who have known you for years and who can speak to your *honesty, integrity, ethics*, etc. Don't be afraid to go to them.

Magic Bullets

A final word before we start our journey: Like almost anything in life, the perfect solution is often found better in concept than in practice. Put another way, there are few if any "magic bullets" that can pinpoint the ideal job or the perfect

way to land it. Even if you follow every piece of advice in this

book - or any other, for that matter – chances are you will still

find yourself coming up with the short straw more often than

you'd like. Before you get depressed over the inevitable

rejections, however, consider these facts:

- The U.S. Navy's crack flight team, the Blue Angels,
  always videotape their performances and analyze
  everything right down to how the pilots walk out onto
  the tarmac before the show begins. And even after
  years and years of training and experience, they will all
  admit to never having had a flawless event – someone
  is always out of step by half a second, too quick with a
  salute, or a hair off on a flight turn or other acrobatic
  movement. Perfection is a goal, not an achievement.
- Statistics vary, but the average salesman can normally
  expect to make 10 or 20 – calls for every single lead he

or she generates – and of those leads, only 1 out of every 10 may result in an actual sale. In other words, think of having to make almost 100 calls before getting a single closing. This is what it means to handle rejection. Think about this when you're sending out resumes and waiting for the phone to ring.

- Babe Ruth, who held the record for the most home runs in a single season until Hank Aaron shattered his record, struck out 1,330 times in his life. If we do the math, this means that he missed the ball completely at least five or six times for each one when he knocked it out of the park.

- Michael Jordan, perhaps the greatest basketball player of his generation during his time with the Chicago Bulls, confessed to missing more than nine thousand baskets, losing more than 300 games over the course of his career, and being tasked with sinking the game-winning shot more than two dozen times only to fall short; yet one can hardly imagine any player in the NBA or any other sport who would not gladly trade their averages for his.

The point is, even if you do everything absolutely and positively right, circumstances beyond your control will still undermine you and torpedo your efforts more often than you would like. Maybe you left with plenty of time to get to an interview but got stuck in the worst traffic jam of the year and wound up arriving late. Maybe your interviewer got up on the wrong side of bed and is in a foul mood that you can't fix or overcome. Maybe the hiring manager has an ax to grind and is only interested in finding someone who shares his or her particular beef with the world or who wants a friend s/he can go to lunch with rather than a rising star. Stuff happens.

Speaking of which, Or maybe you were already running late to an interview and ran out the door only to find as you got to the subway that the foul smell you noticed on the way down the escalator was…the dog's calling card you somehow stepped in with your brand new shoes that you bought specifically for your interview. (Side note: This actually did happen to a friend of this author.) Failure, like the proverbial dog dropping, *simply happens*. You can either accept the fact that you will, more likely than not, have to undergo several interviews before getting an offer (and likely several offers before finding the "right" job) or you can let the inevitable failures crush your spirit.

But doing the latter means your search will take longer.

Takeaway Points

- *Understand that things have changed.* You're not in Kansas anymore, and from this point on things are going to be very, very different from the world you've known up until now. You will be judged much more quickly – and much less fairly – because people will not have the time to get to know the real you. Instead, they will make observations and conclusions based on their observations and how those match with their own experiences. Get used to being treated unfairly.

- *Always leave as little as possible to chance.* This means putting your best foot forward and coming across as professionally as possible, even if it means sacrificing some aspects of your personal appearance that you treasure.

- *Spring for some decent clothes and at least one good business suit.* Even though business casual is considered the norm, you first have to land the job before you can "afford" to be casual.

- *Expect some setbacks.* It's impossible to say you'll never get discouraged, but disappointment is inevitable as part of the job search process. Learning to deal with the inevitable disappointments will go a long way toward helping you persevere.

SELF-ASSESSING

*"I never desire to converse with a man who
has written more than he has read."*

- *Samuel Johnson*

B efore starting your search, you first need to answer the inevitable question: "Okay, *what is it I really want to do?*" Your answers may vary from "becoming an engineer" to something as simple as "finding a part-time entry level slot that will get me out from under my parents' house." But as anal-retentive as it might sound, figuring out what you want to do before starting your search can actually go a long way toward helping you narrow your focus and – ironically – reduce the amount of time it takes to find a job.

Far too many people, when asked why they went to work for a particular firm – even people who might have been with a company for 20-30 years – all too often say, "Well, it was a job…" (These are also often the same people who are miserable in their jobs and who are bound to make *your* life miserable as well if you wind up working for them.) Taking a position to get your foot in the door or to provide a much-needed paycheck to cover the bills so you can put a roof over your head are fine, but in the long run, leaping without looking often means landing someplace that you don't want to be or that will, in a surprisingly short time, wear out its welcome faster than you think.

Suppose we have two recent graduates, Holly and Frank. Both went to the same school and got B.A. degrees and are looking for that first job now that they are out of school.

Holly enjoys theatre and art, but she is also an avid rollerblader who likes being active. Frank enjoys riding his bike from time to time, but his interests tend more toward the political arena and playing video games than competing in triathlons. Both have interned at different offices and waited tables, so they have built up a small savings to cover their initial expenses when they move into friends' apartments and start looking for full-time work. Here's what their target lists might look like:

Holly

Degree: English

Interests

- Talking with people
- Writing and editing
- Theatre

Frank

Degree: History

Interests

- Politics and international affairs

- Climate change

- Computer programming

Given just their different interests, Holly and Frank could consider the possible following career options to start with:

Holly

Interests	Career Options
Talking with people	Public relations
	Marketing
	Sales
	Event planning

Interests	Career Options
Writing and editing	Advertising
	Journalism
	Copyediting
Theatre	Fund raising
	Promotions
	Sales

Frank's interests might be similarly broken down into something along these lines:

Frank

Interests	Career Options
Politics and international affairs	Campaigns
	Commerce
	Business

Interests	Career Options
Climate change	Conservation
	Recycling
Computer programming	Web programmer
	Content manager

Notice how in each instance at this stage, neither Frank nor Holly has tried to determine which of the activities is necessarily a favorite or preferred one; each has simply listed some personal interests and things that they both enjoy doing. Once that is done, they can then brainstorm to see which careers might lend themselves to those different activities or which would make use of particular sets of skills that relate to them. Simply because Frank enjoys playing games or Holly likes going to the museum does not mean that either will wind up doing something in either area, but by writing out some personal interests to help guide them, each is taking a valuable step toward narrowing some possible career options.

Linked Steps

Mapping out possible career options is a good first step, but it's also one that requires keeping a very basic rule in mind. Unfortunately, it is also one of the rules people most often forget when looking for their first or second job out of school. Namely, *each position or job you take invariably starts you down a particular professional path.* Just as the person who takes a job with a company "just to get a job" might eventually find himself or herself "trapped" after several years – the money is good, changing positions might mean taking a cut in salary or going back to school, etc.– so new graduates can easily find themselves quickly moving down a highway that, if they are not careful, will lead them further and further from where they really want to go.

Suppose Holly decides that she really wants to be a journalist. Maybe she even did a little work on the college newspaper and her high school yearbook, and she is still in touch with her old teacher who ran the yearbook program. She puts together a resume outlining her skills and reaches out for a reference but finds that, lacking an internship or any professional experience, no one wants to hire her. Too many competitors, it turns out, have internships and more professional experience. Desperate to get out from her parents' house, she takes a job working as a museum assistant doing cataloguing work for exhibits. The work isn't glamorous, but is provides a steady paycheck and gives her a means of paying her bills. Did she make the right call?

One could answer yes or no, but in truth, she has already taken a step that is moving her further away from her goal. If Holly's only aim is to land a job that will afford her some freedom and mobility before she heads back to graduate school in a couple of years to earn a master's degree, then spending one or two years in a grunt job might be just what she wants. However, the more time she spends doing museum work, the more experience she will develop in a field that she likes but not necessarily one she wants to do for the rest of her life. Put another way, if Holly really wants to be a journalist, she will undoubtedly find it a lot more difficult to transition into a journalism job after working three years in a museum - possibly with a promotion or two under her belt as well - when she winds up competing with people who already have one or two years of journalism experience. Even more challenging: the money she's likely to make as an entry-level reporter may not compare all that favorably to the money she makes at the museum. It may still be possible for her to switch careers, but the transition will now be a lot more difficult than it would have been had she held out a bit longer two or three years back.

The main point to remember is that every decision you make is *inevitably linked to others we will have to make somewhere down the line*. When you graduate, life is a hallway of open doors to the future; you can pick and choose which ones you want to enter and explore. (Side note: This is perhaps the greatest reason many older people all too often envy and resent their younger colleagues.) But whichever career path we inevitably decide to follow eventually makes switching gears later on all the more difficult. We soon learn new skills and abilities, we start earning steady (and hopefully greater) paychecks along the way, and before too long, we find ourselves in a comfort zone that is very difficult to leave. In this sense, selecting a career path is a lot like choosing how to cross a stream: There are a variety of stepping-stones we might select; but once we take a few steps, we've begun to commit ourselves to a particular path. Granted, if we change our minds, we can still go back try another route, but our journey will take longer as a result. Even more worrisome, the longer we spend changing courses and trying different paths, the greater our chances of sooner or later slipping and falling.

Okay, let's say Holly takes the job at the museum and then goes back to school three years later and earns her master's degree in creative writing. The program takes eighteen months. Now she not only has another degree (along with some hefty student loans), but the only job she's likely to be qualified for based on her three years of professional experience and almost two more of additional schooling is…another museum job. She may be able to land another job with a local newspaper based on her writing training, but chances are the paper is going to be more interested in someone with actual experience vs. academic credentials. The pay she is likely to get will also probably be a lot smaller since she'll be starting at a lower position without the necessary experience to command a higher salary. Even worse, she may have to take a second job because her student loans now make taking the reporter job by itself impossible. Her journey across the stream has now gotten a lot more difficult.

Frank, on the other hand, follows a slightly different course. Like Holly, he's unsure at graduation what he really wants to do but decides to pursue two possible options. He enjoys working on the Web and has a passion for environmental issues, but he can't find an environmental organization in his area that will hire him. So, he takes a job doing Web design for the county school system while still reaching out and making connections to some environmental groups he knows. It's not an ideal situation, but the work relates to something he likes doing and which will hopefully help him build some solid skills. After eight months, one of the organizations he has kept in touch with develops an opening that fits his skills. By leveraging his experience in a related area, he's managed to keep his main goal in focus, and now he's able to step into something more to his liking.

Granted, he may return to graduate school in a few years like

Holly, but for now, the course he has followed has kept him in

the right direction and also saved him a great deal of

frustration. And it's also made stepping back or reversing

course unnecessary.

Now ask yourself: Which person would you rather be

more like, Frank or Holly?

The C.O.F.F.E.E. Approach

Let's say you've made your list of different areas of

interest and decided which field(s) you want to pursue. The

next step is to hop online and start looking for jobs, right?

Wrong. Statistically speaking, very few jobs actually

ever make the listings in the online job sections (if that many).

Moreover, of those that do make it to the streets, far too many

are often already filled by internal candidates or people who have connections to the company and its hiring managers. The job may sound like the perfect opportunity for you, but chances are someone in the company is probably recommending a friend or former co-worker, and in the grand scheme, that person has a leg up on you in terms of getting that all-important first foot in the door.

Think of it this way: If you spend 90% of your job search applying for positions online, you're spending 90% of your time chasing *maybe* 10-15 percent (or fewer) of the jobs that are out there (and with an even smaller chance at success.) Blindly applying to ad after ad after ad is not only a highly inefficient way of finding a job, it's also one that inevitably costs you significant amounts of time, effort, and frustration with very little in the way of potential return.

But there's an even bigger reason not to rely too heavily on online advertising for your job search. One of the dirty secrets of recruiting is that many firms run position listings year-round *not* because they have positions to fill but because *they simply want to fill their talent pools.* In other words, that fantastic job you saw that looked as though it would be an ideal match? There may not be a job behind it at all; the firm simply wants to collect more resumes for similar positions to make sure there are sufficient numbers of updated resumes on file in case they company decides to hire for something like this *in the future.* Even companies that are in hiring freezes and have no plans to fill any new openings may run advertisements if for no other reason than because they are contractually obligated with some online search sites to run a certain number of advertisements throughout the year. They can also be advertising to keep tabs on salary expectations and software skills that are current in the market. The bottom line? Don't expect many ad listings to have actual positions behind them that you can interview for.

This is not to suggest you should never use online advertisements as part of your job search; but just to be sure when applying that you keep a measured perspective. But remember, for every person who finds a job through an advertisement, far greater numbers find them through personal contacts, networking connections, and similar means.

Which brings us to your homework. Before you start applying for particular positions or companies, stop and see what connections you may have to that company or firm. Chances are you may know someone who knows someone (or who knows someone who knows someone, etc.) who may be able to put in a word for you at a company you're targeting.

Sounds good, but how do you go about finding that person? By utilizing your network of Colleagues, Organizations, Friends/Family, and Everyone Else (COFFEE).

Colleagues – These can be just about anyone you've ever played, studied, or worked with. They can include former teammates, co-workers, study hall mentors, tutors, volunteer coordinators, church contacts, or anybody else outside your immediate social circle. Play on a college softball or soccer team? Participate in any get-out-the-vote campaigns or charity drives? Kept in touch with your RA from sophomore year? Chances are someone somewhere whose path crossed yours probably has a connection to that firm or knows someone who does. And reaching out to them to build your network list will do far more to position you effectively than any amount of blind letter writing and resume forwarding.

Organizations – Did you belong to any civic groups while in school? Were you in the boy/girl scouts growing up? Is there an alumni chapter from your college in your area? Does a friend have a local church youth group that keeps an online bulletin board for people looking for help? All of these are potential sources of connections who can help you toward getting your foot in the door.

Okay, you say, but suppose I spent my college years more in pursuit of what we'll politely call "recreational activities" instead of networking ones? What if my expertise was more in the area of keg tapping and twelve-ounce curls on Friday and Saturday nights? Admittedly, you'll probably have your work cut out for you if you don't have any fallback groups, but almost any city or town has a local networking chapter of professionals seeking to connect with one another and share tips and leads. Consider:

- Is there a professional society in your area?

- Is there a Meetup group that meets every month?

- Do any community-focused organizations plan and sponsor events in your area?

- Is there a local Toastmasters organization you might join?

Some of these may seem quaint in many respects, but bear in mind that they also represent opportunities to establish connections with people who may have contacts in their own network who can help you. Put another way, if you have never done any networking or volunteer work in these areas, this may be the time to come out of your shell. Even if no connections come up initially, over time your network will expand through these people and – more likely than not – eventually lead to some kind of contact who has the sort of connection you're looking for. Your challenge is to start the process and then have the patience and perseverance to see it through.

Friends – This is by far your most valuable network. A simple mathematical illustration clearly demonstrates just how effective your network of friends can be. Using the famous six-degrees-of-separation example (i.e., that everyone on the planet can be connected through just six acquaintances – think of "Six Degrees of Kevin Bacon"), let's go back and look at Holly and Frank. Assume Frank has just six close friends from high school or college and that each of them has six friends as

42

well. Let's further suppose that Holly, who is just slightly more extroverted than Frank because of her rollerblading group, has just two more close friends in her network. What we might see would be something like this:

Frank						
1st	(Sue)	(Carl)	(Elle)	(Ken)	(Fred)	(Chris)
2nd	6	6	6	6	6	6
3rd	36	36	36	36	36	36
4th	216	216	216	216	216	216
5th	1,296	1,296	1,296	1,296	1,296	1,296
6th	7,776	7,776	7,776	7,776	7,776	7,776
Total:	9,331	9,331	9,331	9,331	9,331	9,331
Grand Total:	55,986					

Holly								
1st	(Sue)	(Carl)	(Elle)	(Ken)	(Fred)	(Chris)	(Sally)	(Fran)
2nd	6	6	6	6	6	6	6	6
3rd	36	36	36	36	36	36	36	36
4th	216	216	216	216	216	216	216	216
5th	1,296	1,296	1,296	1,296	1,296	1,296	1,296	1,296
6th	7,776	7,776	7,776	7,776	7,776	7,776	7,776	7,776
Total:	9,331	9,331	9,331	9,331	9,331	9,331	9,331	9,331
Grand Total:	74,648							

Notice that by simply adding just two more friends, Holly increases her six-degrees-of-separation network by 33%. In other words, just knowing two more people has the potential to expand her network by one-third.

Admittedly, this example is more illustrative than practical – no one besides a professional politician would have the time or willingness to rush out and be expected to shake hands with thousands of potential contacts – but the point is that *each additional contact has the potential to significantly expand your network*, often in ways we will never fully see or understand. This is why your network of friends will always be your most powerful resource when looking for connections.

Family – Much like friends, family members provide essential contacts to people when it comes to helping them get started. Consider:

- George Will, the famous columnist and book author, got his start in journalism with the help of a family friend.

- Bill Lawrence, the creator of such sitcoms as *Scrubs* and *Cougar Town*, had a family friend in the television business who helped him get started as a scriptwriter and – eventually – a show developer and executive producer.

- Jennifer Anniston, star of *Friends* and multiple movies, was god-daughter of Telly Savalas, the actor who played *Kojak* in the 1970s.

Even for those of us who don't have family connections that extend into Hollywood, Washington, DC, and the recording industry, chances are someone in your parents' circle of friends or brothers'/sisters' circle has connections that can help put you in touch with someone who may be able to get your foot in the door. Don't waste potential connections that could save you invaluable amounts of time and effort simply because you're hesitant to reach out to mom and dad or that distant aunt or uncle. Swallowing some pride now may save you weeks of frustration later if it helps put you on a path toward making the connection that helps you get a job.

Reaching Out

Once you have identified a group of people to contact, you need to start framing your pitch. Just as every sales professional knows that most sales are won or lost in the first few moments, so yours needs to be quick, pointed, and thorough.

In most cases, a brief e-mail is an excellent way to break the ice, but like anything, there are more wrong ways than right ones to come across to someone. Generally, each outreach should include five basic steps:

- A polite introduction giving the person your name, your background, and how you obtained this person's name

- A quick outline of your background and experience (no more than one or two sentences)

- An explanation of the type of position you are searching for

- An indication you know something about the company and have looked into it before contacting the source

- A proactive offer to follow up and reward the person for his or her help (this is probably the one item that is most frequently overlooked)

As mentioned previously, this may seem self-evident at first, but a quick conversation with almost any hiring manager will quickly tell you that a surprising number of applicants and potential candidates fail in a number of these areas. For instance, compare the two pitches below:

To: Joe Jobholder

From: Jim Jobseeker

Hi, Joe –

I understand from Alice Alumni that your a graduate of Templetown University and work at Finer Company, Inc. I graduated with a degree in economics and am looking for a job in the area. Can you let me know if Finer is hiring? My e-mail is jimjobseeker@email.com.

Thanks!

JJ

What's wrong with this e-mail? Several things:

- **It doesn't include a proper introduction or explanation.** Jim not only has not introduced himself, but he also didn't really give Joe much information about how he got his name from Alice. A little politeness goes a long way, and in this case, Jim's already put himself behind before getting started.

- **The opening sentence includes a blatant error.** Jim said "your" instead of "you're." Again, this may seem nitpicky, but it probably does not inspire much confidence see such a notable mistake in an opening line. Even worse, Joe's probably not going to be inclined to pass along the name of someone he hardly knows and whose only interaction shows a lack of attention to detail.

- **Jim clearly failed to do his homework.** Asking if Joe's company is hiring is something Jim could find out on his own with just a few minutes of searching on the Internet. What kind of position is he looking for? Does he have any idea which position(s) would be a good match for his interests and goals? By not being specific, he has further undermined his standing in Joe's eyes.

- **He did not offer anything of value in exchange for her help.** One hand always washes the other when networking, and Jim's only real message here is "What can you do to help me?" rather than offering to *work together* with Joe. Taken on top of the other errors already mentioned, Jim has struck out before really even getting up to bat.

Now, compare Jim's e-mail pitch to Julie's:

To: Francis Foundjob

From: Julie Needajob

Hi, Francis –

My name is Julie Needajob, and I'm a fellow graduate of Templetown University. Alice Alumni gave me your name and suggested that I get in touch with you about some openings at Finer Things, Inc. I noticed from the Web site that Finer Things is looking for an editor, and I believe my experience on the campus newspaper and online magazine would make me an excellent match for the job. Would there be some time next week to talk or perhaps get together for coffee? I can be reached at julieneedajob@email.com.

Thanks for your help. I will look forward to talking with you!

Sincerely,

Julie Needajob

What did Julie do right in her e-mail?

- **She gave a proper introduction.** Not only did Julie introduce herself, but she also let Francis know immediately how she got her name and provided some important information about their shared background at Templetown. Even though it may not be strong at this point, she's at least established some kind of connection to her contact.

- **She clearly did her homework.** Rather than simply asking if Finer Things is hiring, Julie specifically identified the type of position she was looking for. Francis now has an idea of Julie's aims and expectations in addition to knowing more about her.

- **She gave a brief mention of her experience and qualifications.** Julie indicated the position she was looking for, but notice how she also mentioned how her background and experience would fit the job.

- **She politely offered to follow up and connect informally.** Assuming Francis accepts Julie's offer, she has made an inside connection at the company for the cost of simply buying someone else a cup of coffee. And, not to be overlooked -

- **Her e-mail was free of any glaring spelling errors or typos.** Granted, this is probably far more important for a detail-oriented job like editing, but as noted earlier,

she has left very little to chance.

Now, comparing the e-mail that Julie forwarded to the one that

Jim sent, ask yourself this question: Based on just the general

tone and overall accuracy of both messages, which one would

you be more likely to forward?

The Pros and Cons of Templates

Given the enormous volume of e-mails, text messages, letters,

and other correspondence that is associated with any job

search, it is easy to think your life will be substantially easier if

you have some kind of "boilerplate" or "standard" text blurb

that you can cut and paste in to save yourself time.

There are sound reasons for and against this idea. On

the one hand, it allows you to save time and not have to

reinvent the wheel each time you want to contact a particular

prospect or highlight your qualifications. On the other hand, it's very easy to overlook specific information that you need to change when customizing a template for a particular recipient. You have to find/change all instances of the addressee's name, the company name, and probably some aspects of your background that you want to highlight or omit depending on the job.

A good way to guard against this is to start with a standard template that has blank underlined areas inserted for any sections you need to specifically customize. By using this instead of copying and pasting a previous e-mail, you greatly reduce the risk of inadvertently forwarding the wrong wording to the prospect:

Here's one example:

To: _____
From: Julie Needajob
Hi, _____ –

My name is Julie Needajob, and I'm a fellow graduate of Templetown University. _____ gave me your name and suggested that I get in touch with you about some openings at

_____. I noticed from the Web site that _____ is looking

for an _____, and I believe my experience

_____ and _____ would make

me an excellent match for the job. Would there be some time

next week to talk or perhaps get together for coffee? I can be

reached at julieneedajob@email.com.

Thanks for your help. I will look forward to talking with you!

Sincerely,

Julie Needajob

Having a proofed-and-ready template helps ensure not only

that Julie's content has a better chance at being error-free, but

the inserted blanks require her to customize the text for each

prospect she contacts. In this way, it acts as a "check" against

mistakenly overlooking any copy that needs to be changed or

updated.

Tracking

Once you start reaching out to your contacts – particularly as your network expands – it becomes increasingly difficult to keep track of all the names and their respective affiliations. You may remember Fred, the business associate of your cousin Sally, who said he had a friend named Jim whose company was looking to hire somebody, but if a month or two goes by before you hear anything, you're going to be hard pressed to remember Fred if he emails you out of the blue about a possible opportunity. Moreover, fumbling while you try and remember his name certainly won't win you any brownie points on the phone or help you if you take too much time to place his name.

Enter your tracking system. By keeping some kind of log entry or job diary, you can note not only the names of the people you contact but also outline some quick notes about how you know person, how you heard about him or her, and what issues or items you will want to remember when talking with them. While there are certainly myriad ways to track this, two particular methods stand out: the spreadsheet method and the job diary.

Spreadsheets

Recording names, addresses, and other contact information on an Excel spreadsheet is an excellent way of keeping all the various people straight in your network. Even better, many networking Web sites, such as Linked In and others, allow you to download your connections into a data file that you can then pull into an Excel document for formatting. This gives you an instant glimpse of the people in your network, where they work, and their contact information.

Your spreadsheet can be formatted any number of ways and set up to include a variety of relevant data, but most should include the following at a minimum:

- The name of the contact (spelled correctly)

- The name of his or her company

- Relevant contact information (phone, e-mail, etc.)

- Alternate contact information (preferred contact address, etc.)

- The date you reached out to the person

- A short blurb about how you know them

A sample tracking spreadsheet might look something like this:

Last Name	First Name	Employer	E-mail	Follow-up
Alton	Denise	Digital Visual	denise.alton @gmail.com	Made note to email on 3/10.
Abrams	Robert	Alpine Digital	rabrams@alp inedigital.com	Scheduled coffee for 3/20
Aston	Philip	Housing and Develop-ment Office	palbertson@ housing.gov	Made note to email on 3/22.

Remember, spreadsheets can be formatted not only to include the listed information but also allow the searcher to record small bits of information and update them over time. If this seems over the top to you, remember that most companies track sales leads in just this manner – and your number one job in searching for your job is *to sell yourself.*

Job Diary

While the spreadsheet format offers a number of benefits, the constant shifting of cells and text can be troubling for some. Maybe your experience with spreadsheets isn't particularly strong or your eyes glaze over at the site of cell after cell after cell of different data. For those whose inclinations run more toward the printed word rather than numerals, the job diary is often an equally effective way of tracking your outreach efforts.

Much like the spreadsheet, the job diary allows you to list the relevant information and to search it at a moment's notice in the event you need to find a contact's name or recall how and why you reached out to that particular individual. Like the spreadsheet option, the job diary should the same information, but it can be formatted much more creatively. A typical listing might be formatted in the following manner:

June 20

- E-mailed Jack Johnson (jjohnson@MDI.com) at Middle Data International re: possible systems integration assistant position. (Jack is friend of Allison McHale from school). Mentioned IT background from summer internship.

- Called Elle Richardson (erichardson@exceptionalones.com) re: IT opening at Exceptional Systems, Inc. Mentioned that I was an alum of Middletown University and was looking for openings in the area and would be willing to work with her if she was trying to fill other positions in her firm.

- Sent text message to Richard Roberts (friend of Susan Roper – rroberts@gmail.com) re: getting together for coffee. He says his firm has no openings at present but wants to keep in touch. Suggested getting together next week for coffee.

Notice how each listing involves at most two or three sentences and contains the contact name, a brief mention of how the searcher knows the person, and any other relevant contact information. If in the next week or two a contact responds, the searcher can go into the diary and run a quick search for the person's name and within seconds find the relevant information needed to ensure a positive conversation with the contact. He can also access the contact's e-mail address immediately to help save time on preparing any follow-up correspondence. When a contact does reach out, the searcher can then record the date and time that the two met for coffee or lunch, as well as noting any bits of information that might be relevant for future discussions.

Best of all, the searcher made a point of offering to help at least one of the contacts in case *they* were looking for something. This kind of helpful approach – what can I do for *you* while we're networking? – will very likely go over much better than the more familiar, "Are you hiring right now?" slant. Think about it: This person probably gets several e-mails like this a month if not every week, so whatever makes your pitch stand out from the rest goes a long way toward eliciting a response and establishing that all-critical connection.

Networking vs. Job Hunting

Admittedly, it's easy when searching for a job to forget that *the process takes time*. Suppose you e-mail several dozen people and find that none of them are hiring at the moment – do you move on and keep searching elsewhere or make an effort to keep in touch in the weeks and months ahead?

Again, experience shows that what is perhaps the most obvious answer is the one most seldom practiced. Ask anyone who's heard from a job seeker and told him or her that there weren't any openings if he or she ever heard from that person again. Chances are the answer is negative. It's for this reason that you need to remember that while your ultimate goal may be to land a job somewhere, your *more immediate goal* is to establish a network of connections that you can stay in touch with over time so you'll be in a position to benefit when something opens up (which admittedly could be in several weeks or several months).

Sounds good, you say, but how can I make sure I do this? Even professionals who have been in the workforce for two or three decades aren't always able to meticulously follow up as much or as readily as they would like. They make mental notes to drop lines to people from time to time but then, over time, inevitably forget to follow up or stay in touch, and before long, the connection fizzles. If something opens up that a connection hears about, the chances of him or her following up with you without that relationship and steady contact is minimal at best.

But how to do this without becoming a pest? It's one thing to reach out to someone from time to time, but calling or e-mailing every other week probably means you're more likely to annoy the source than elicit help or leads. So, what do you do?

The answer is surprisingly simple. As anyone who has ever done any cold-calling sales can relate, it's all goes back to how you track the contacts you've made. (And if you're among the fortunate who have been spared the joys of cold calling, pat yourself on the back and count yourself among the lucky.) The best way is often the simplest one: just make a reminder on your calendar program to follow up with the contact in a few weeks' time. Top salespeople who reach out to potential clients and get a polite response (as opposed to someone slamming down the phone) often go directly to their business calendar or whichever program they use to track prospects and jump ahead to a date some time in the near future. They then add a reminder to follow up with the contact, making sure to list his/her company, contact info, and what was discussed the last time they spoke. Several weeks later, when they log into their computer, up pops the reminder to reach back out and stay in touch.

But what do I say, you ask? How do you follow up an earlier contact with something other than simply, "Hi, it's me. I'm still looking for a job. Has anything changed?" Here is where you really have to be on your toes. If you know *anything* about the contact – a sports interest, hobby, or even a professional interest – this is the time to tie that into your

message. Consider the following two e-mails:

To: Jack Jobholder

From: Jerome Jobseeker

Re: Job Search

Hi, Jack –

My Outlook calendar reminded me that I should follow up with

you this week to see if anything's changed at Hiring People,

Inc. Can you let me know when you get a chance? My e-mail

is jackjobholder@gmail.net.

Thanks.

Jerome

Now this one on the facing page:

To: Jack Jobholder

From: Julie Jobseeker

Re: Keeping in Touch

Hi, Jack –

I just realized it's been a few weeks since we connected, so I just wanted to reach out to make sure we stay in touch. I happened to catch this article in last week's paper about some of the ways to correct a bad golf swing – mine can certainly use some help! – so I wanted to be sure to pass it along since I remember you were looking forward to getting out on the links this summer, too.

Hope all is well – keep in touch!

Best,

Julie

PS – I saw Hiring People, Inc. has an opening for an editorial assistant. Let me know if there would be some time on your calendar next week for us to talk. :-)

Notice the difference in tone between the two e-mails. The first clearly indicates why the job seeker is contacting the source, but he comes across as matter-of-fact and too what's-in-it-for-me. ("My Outlook reminds me to contact you...") While he may win points for directness, his people skills and source interest clearly need improvement. If Jack begins to feel his only worth is as a job resource rather than a person, he's far less likely to offer any help.

In contrast, the second e-mail comes over as upbeat and positive. Even better, the job seeker has remembered something about her source and made an effort to include it in the e-mail. She also listed the job she noticed on the Web site as an almost-afterthought but kept the pitch breezy and light. Sure, her contact undoubtedly realizes the true purpose of her e-mail, but he will also notice the extra length she went to in order to provide him with something of value as opposed to simply asking outright if anything had changed since their last conversation. (Her referencing the Web site also indicates once again she did more homework than her counterpart.) Given these differences, it's probably not too difficult to guess which seeker is more likely to receive a reply from Jack.

The bottom line: *Always be thinking ahead when reaching out to potential contacts.* Your goal may be to get a job in the long run, but in the short it should be to grow your network as far and wide as possible so you can snare those leads when they come out.

"It always surprises me how many people who have been in the workforce for years fail to apply the rules of simple common courtesy," one Web developer said. "I worked with this one woman for years before we were both laid off, and after sending her some e-mails to keep in touch and checkup, I never heard anything back from her. Six months later, she e-mails me out of the blue asking if I will be a reference for her on a job interview she has *that day*. I reluctantly said yes, but I never got a call or so much as a thank you from her. When she did the same thing again a few weeks later, I deleted her message and never replied – and this was a woman who had spent *more than a decade in marketing*."

Never forget the importance of simple courtesy – a little of it can go a very long way.

Takeaway Points

- *Think carefully about what you want before taking a job.* Far too many people take positions just to "have a job" only to find themselves unhappy at best or miserable at worst after only a few weeks or months. Spending some time looking now before leaping later can save you lots of time and frustration.

- *Remember your COFFEE.* Whether reaching out to contacts, organizations, friends and family, or anyone else you know, never forget that your contacts will serve you better when it comes to networking.

- *Never forget that all decisions are "linked" decisions, often in ways we won't and can't possibly foresee.* Any choice we make between a given set of options means choosing a direction that leads us down a particular path; and reversing course, while initially possible, becomes increasingly costly and more time consuming the further down the path we go. Taking the time to ask yourself where something can lead does not by necessarily guarantee a successful outcome, but it can go a long way toward helping avoid costly mistakes.

- *Always track your outreach efforts and the contacts that you make.* You'll want to be able to recall whom you spoke with and how you know them when the call comes through or an e-mail lands in your inbox.

- *Be patient but persistent.* Just because someone doesn't have an opening at the moment doesn't mean he or she won't have one in a few months. Staying in touch with someone over several months can actually save you time in the long run if something opens up after a few months with someone you've kept in steady contact with as opposed to spending a year talking only with people who have openings at the time you reach out to them. Remember the rules of common courtesy, because the dividends they pay can be substantial; just as the penalties for neglecting them can be as well.

PREPARING THE RESUME

"Writing is manual labor of the mind: a job, like laying pipe."

- *John Gregory Dunne*

O kay, let's assume you've identified some areas of personal interest and found a contact who's willing to help you get connected with a company. "Send me your resume," she says cheerfully. "I'll forward it to HR." All set, right?

Not really. Gone are the days – if they ever truly existed – where one type of resume suited all hiring purposes. In the technological era, your resume not only has to reflect a

73

particular set of skills and abilities, it also has to demonstrate

cultural compatibility with the organization. This means that

you can't simply attach a generic resume, forward it, and hope

you'll land an interview. You have to go a lot further.

This is where people who have been out of the job hunt

themselves can sometimes be less than helpful without

meaning any harm. Suppose your contact is someone who has

spent several years with this particular firm. Chances are, she

tends – consciously or not – to see things through the prism of

that organization and how it operates. Culturally, her company

has a particular perspective on what it expects from its

employees and how it views the world, and if your resume does

not reflect a compatible outlook, either because of its wording,

its format, or some other reason, you're far more likely to end

up missing out than getting in. If your contact works at a law

or accounting firm, for instance, hiring managers there very

likely expect a heavy degree of conformity and professionalism as compared to a start-up operation or dot-com, where such "stodginess" and conservatism will probably reflect more negatively than positively on your chances.

But even more than appearing a certain way to match the culture of the company, your resume also needs to be *customized to reflect the position for which you are applying.* If you have a copy of the job description for that particular company, you're going to need to take some time to revise your resume to highlight the skills that are required for the job. Simply e-mailing a generic summary of your skills and abilities or pasting the job description into your resume may get you into the company database, but it won't be nearly as likely to get your name pulled on any searches for qualified personnel.

At one time, you could be guaranteed that your resume would receive – at most – 30 seconds when read by an HR representative. In today's job market, however, *it's not likely to get even that* if it isn't specialized to reflect the position you want. Why? Because nowadays resumes aren't even reviewed by people; they're scanned by applicant tracking software (ATS) packages that help companies weed out those that contain insufficient numbers of key terms or "buzzwords" for a particular position.

Think of it as being like an intra-corporate Google search. You send your resume to your contact, who forwards it to HR. When it lands in the HR reps' inbox, she is more than likely going to put it into a pool of other available resumes and then, when the time comes to pull resumes for an open position, do a search that scans the resumes using a specialized software package designed to pick out keywords like, "accounts" and "costs" and "expenses" and "receivables" and "payable" to name a few. Once the scans are complete, each resume will then be assigned a percentage score, and those meeting a particular threshold will be pulled for further review and possible forwarding to the hiring manager. If the resume you forwarded is too generic or doesn't include the right set of "buzzwords," it will never make the cutoff – and you will not be contacted for an interview.

"It really astounds me sometimes how out of touch some people can be when it comes to putting resumes together," says one forty-year old job seeker. "People who have been working in certain positions for 10 or 20 years forget what it's like to be out in the job market. They really have no clue how cutthroat it can be or how hard it is to specialize your resume for a particular position."

Resume Writing 101

When putting a resume together, there are a certain number of rules that have to be followed regardless of the kind of job they're aimed for. Times and trends may change, but each resume more or less must do the following:

Tell a story – Simply summarizing a set of responsibilities you had from an earlier job does not cut it. Managers are looking to see what *contributions* you made to your last organization and how you helped it grow and improve. Even if your last job was working as a barista at the college coffee shop, you'll need to indicate how your role made a difference in the organization. Did you reduce cash register errors? Make a point of improving customer service? Order replacement materials earlier to avoid empty bins or run-outs of available flavors? Solve difficult employee problems or meet demanding customers' expectations? These are the kinds of things managers want to see, not just a recapitulation of what you were responsible for doing.

Contain quantified achievements – Listing a set of bullet points outlining how you improved something is certainly helpful, but the next logical question a manager is going to ask is, "How do you know this? By how much did you improve this while working at this particular job?" The more you can put numbers behind your achievements – even if they are estimated percentages – the better your position will be vs. someone who *doesn't* quantify his or her accomplishments. In general, those that are most significant and relevant to the position should be the ones listed first; those that cannot be quantified or which do not represent major accomplishments should be relegated to the middle or bottom of the list.

Be free of spelling and grammatical mistakes of any kind – Common sense tells us that this should go without saying, but once again, any conversation with a hiring manager or recruiter tells us otherwise. In an age of ubiquitous spell-check programs, such errors are not only inexcusable but also the kiss of death for someone trying to make a positive impression. (This is especially true if the job you're applying for has a publishing angle…). "You get one chance to make a first impression with me," says one recruiter. "And if I see that you can't be bothered to check your resume for common mistakes and spelling errors, how am I going to look forwarding that to my boss or a hiring manager?"

Another manager put it even more bluntly: "If you're lucky," he said. "A spelling error will just get your resume thrown away immediately." And if you're not lucky? "If you're not lucky, someone will put a post-it note on your resume highlighting the mistake and it will be forwarded around the office so people can laugh at you." Don't take a chance on being the butt of an inter-office joke – proof your resume over and over until you're absolutely sure it's free of mistakes. Then run the spell-check. Then, as a final step, *have a friend or family member look it over* just in case you missed anything or something got by the spell-check program. If this seems over-the-top, remember the difference between *pubic relations* and *public relations*. Both terms will pass a spell check, but only one is probably the one you want to highlight (depending on the job).

QUARAMS

No, this isn't a misspelling of the minimum people needed to call a vote; this is the mnemonic device to use when preparing your resume. No matter what kind of position you're applying for, each resume you send out should follow these five basic steps:

*QUA*ntify the achievements that you made

*R*elate the proactive steps you took in your job to improve things and make a difference (vs. "just doing your job")

*A*void personal interests and mission statements (these are considered "filler" items and won't be scanned for keywords)

*M*ake Sure your spelling is 100% accurate

Take a look at the following resume:

JOHN R. DOE

13815 Job Search Lane, Unemployed, Va. 20121 ● 703/555-0306
jdoesit@verizon.net

SUMMARY OF QUALIFICATIONS
- Intern at Data World Consulting
- Earned BA from top-tier college while working full time and combine proven leadership and management experience with team-based environments.

EXPERIENCE

Intern
Data World Consulting
- Responsible for reviewing market research data to identify target segments for various direct mailings, online promotions, and trade show displays/promotions;
- Oversee data-mining initiatives to identify growing or changing market segments in order to revise promotion plans and strategies;
- Identify topics for proposed projects that would best meet the needs of targeted categories and supervise focus groups and survey research to determine potential customer response

- Work as team leader in cross-functional environment to evaluate proposed product lines for feasibility, marketability, cost effectiveness, and risk based on estimated customer counts, projected costs/profits, and past sales/promotion data

Assistant Manager
Coffee Beanery
- Responsible for ensuring sufficient inventory for daily operations of campus coffee shop;
- Drafted work schedules for employees and rotated assignments as necessary to ensure smooth operations;
- Tracked monthly expenses for order evaluations and changes;
- Oversaw entry of expenses into computer database.

EDUCATION
- B.A., Business Administration

Familiar with Microsoft excel, outlook power point, project
Personal interests include biking and triathlons

At first glance, this seems like an impressive resume. The

applicant has had an internship and included recent work

experience that outlines skills that should be relevant to a professional job in an office setting (tracking expenses, overseeing employees, etc.). But on closer look, the resume fails in a number of critical areas:

- **No quantifiable achievements** – All the responsibilities that are listed essentially repeat what could be found on a job description; there is no mention of anything that is quantitatively verifiable.

- **No proactivity** – There is no real accomplishment outlined or improvements that the applicant made in either of the jobs he listed. He merely outlines what his responsibilities were. A manager looking at this has no idea what special contributions this employee made or how he made them.

- **Personal interests** – These are included at the bottom and appear to be placed merely to "fill out" the resume. They are also irrelevant to the position (unless he's applying for the job of coordinating an upcoming athletic event).

- **Spelling mistakes** – Notice that the names of the Microsoft Office software programs are not capitalized. This may seem like a minor infraction, but – again – any error in spelling or punctuation inevitably raises red flags. Also, notice how the first listing contains semicolons at the end of some lines but not others, an inconsistency that will again serve to undermine the applicant's efforts. (Yes, people really do pay attention to this level of detail; it provides an additional level of screening to help reduce the number of applicants for consideration.) If someone has only a few seconds to review your resume, all he or she may really have time to look for aside from a cursory review of your qualifications is to see if you made any common punctuation or consistency mistakes. If you claim to have "strong attention to detail" with some blatant

inconsistencies in your resume – as opposed to the other

person's resume on the manager's desk – guess who's

most likely to be selected for a phone screening?

Now, contrast this with the resume on the following page:

JANE R. DOE

18315 Job Search Lane, Unemployed, Va. 20121 • 703/555-
0306
janedoesit@verizon.net

SUMMARY OF QUALIFICATIONS
- Intern at Worldwide Data Consulting
- Earned BA from top-tier college while working full time and combine proven leadership and management experience with team-based environments.

EXPERIENCE

Intern
Worldwide Data Consulting
- Reviewed market research data to identify target segments for various direct online promotions; identified 26 possible market segments and assisted in creating promotional outreaches for each
- Managed data-mining to identify growing or changing market segments in order to revise promotion plans and strategies
- Proposed 4 projects that met the needs of targeted categories and supervised 4 focus groups to determine customer response rates; achieved response rate improvement of 25%
- Work as team leader for 4 teams in cross-functional environment to evaluate proposed product lines for feasibility, marketability, cost effectiveness

Assistant Manager
Coffee World
- Managed inventory for daily operations of campus coffee shop; successfully reduced shortages by 32%
- Supervised work schedules for employees and rotated assignments as necessary to ensure smooth operations
- Tracked monthly expenses for order evaluations and changes; achieved 10% cost reduction through reduced emergency shipping of foodstuffs to replace depleted inventories
- Managed entry of monthly accounts into computerized database and reduced data errors from 8% to 4.5%

EDUCATION
- B.A., Business Administration

Familiar with Microsoft Excel, Outlook PowerPoint, Project

What did this applicant do right? A number of things:

- **She quantified her achievements** – Even though the listings did not necessarily reflect major changes in terms of profit or cost reduction, she demonstrated the ability to track data and specifically identify what she did.

- **She demonstrated proactivity** – Rather than simply listing her responsibilities, she identified the improvements she made.

- **She did not list any "filler" information** – She kept her resume focused squarely on her accomplishments.

- **She did not have any spelling or formatting mistakes** – All lines are formatted consistently and spelled correctly.

Given these two resumes, which would you be more likely to call in for an interview? Both applicants essentially have the same qualifications and background, and both are the same age with basically the same experience, but one has gone further than the other and given you more information to get a fuller understanding of her capabilities.

Admittedly, it can be difficult to quantify all of our achievements – even vice presidents and managers with 20 years of professional experience have to sit down and go over their

contributions to determine where they made a difference and by

how much their – but the important thing is not so much to have

a number beside every listing *but to be able to explain how you*

determined the number and what difference it made. This is

what prospective employers will want to know, and it's what

you'll need to have ready when you land the interview.

A Word on References

Many job-search books recommend having your references

included on your resume or listing "references available upon

request." Generally, most companies expect you to have

references who can speak to your hard work, honesty, and

commitment, so listing them on your resume is in many

respects superfluous. Moreover, listing them essentially invites

the company to call them, which is not necessarily a bad thing

except that if you're applying for different jobs, the people you list are likely to get multiple calls. Not only does this make things difficult for your contacts in terms of knowing which person called when for which job, but by the fourth or fifth call, the experience can become tiresome. Think for a moment: Do you really want a tired person on the other end of the line recommending you?

This is not to suggest that you shouldn't have a handy list of between three and five people that you can provide a prospective employer, only that you don't want to provide more information than you have to, and you *definitely* don't want to overburden people who are trying to help you. It is also not uncommon for companies to ask for references but not actually get around to calling them due to pressures and time constraints. Some might – and if they ask, you should definitely assume that they will – but always keep in mind the importance of limiting your liabilities, which taxing a source can most definitely do.

That said, if a company does request references, list the name, the person's title, and a phone or e-mail number (and make sure to list the one your source prefers). Once this is done, *e-mail or call your referral to let him or her know that a prospective employer will likely be calling.* Give them the name of the company, who it is who is likely to be calling, and give them some context for the call. If you're applying for an entry-level editing position, be sure to ask your sources to speak to your attention to detail, your accuracy, and your superb spelling ability. Applying for an accounting slot? Make sure people are ready to discuss your quantitative skills and familiarity with spreadsheet programs. *Never let a source get blindsided by a phone call*; this puts them at a disadvantage – which doesn't help your chances – and also makes you look bad to the prospective employer and your source.

Lastly, be sure to track who gets called and who doesn't. When all is said and done, you'll want to be sure to thank the people who spoke on your behalf. In many instances, a personal e-mail might do, but to go above and beyond – and to ensure that they'll be ready and willing to be a source for you again in the future – spend the time and money for a stamp and handwritten thank-you note. (For over-the-top references that you know made all the critical difference, add a small gift to show your appreciation. Coffee gift cards are a very inexpensive way to let people know how much you appreciated their help.)

Again, the less you leave to chance, the better your chances for success.

Takeaway Points

- *Remember to tell a story with your resume.* It's not enough to show what you did at your last job; your goal is to let your potential manager have a better idea of *what kinds of things you can do.*

- *Find a way to include some quantifiable information.* This can be difficult since not every job lends itself to easy measurement or numerical tracking. But being able to point to specific ways to you contributed to improving something – even a few little things – can go a long way on your resume to improving your perceived employment value.

- *Be as anal-retentive as you can when proofing your resume.* Proof the document, use the spell-checker, and get another pair of eyes whenever possible. Think of even the most minute typo as a possible kiss of death. Remember, if someone only has 30 seconds to look at your resume and they catch a typo, you've probably missed your chance then and there.

- *Track the people you connect with and make every possible effort to keep in touch with them over time.* Use a calendar program, your smart phone, or an old-fashioned day planner to make the necessary reminders to drop someone a line every so often, making sure to note what you remember about them and whatever interests they have. A few extra steps now can make all the difference later.

YOU'VE GOT AN INTERVIEW – NOW WHAT?

"The tools I need for my work are paper,
tobacco, food, and a little bit of whiskey."

-William Faulkner

I t's finally happened.

After several weeks of revising your resume and carefully recording each person you contact, someone finally gets back to you and asks to set up a phone interview with the possibility of you coming into the office for a face to face interview afterward. Hanging up the phone, you triumphantly pump your fist in the air and feel your palms sweat.

Okay, you think to yourself. *Now what do I do?*

Everything up to this point has been focused on landing this opportunity, but let's face it, with the possible exceptions of matrimony and expiration, few things compare to the stress and uncertainty people feel at a job interview. Should you be formal and reserved, or open and energetic? Professional and conservative, or loose and creative? Do you wear a business suit, or will a jacket and tie be sufficient? What kinds of questions will they ask? What kind should *you* ask? What answers will be positive indicators, and which should be considered warning bells?

As the saying goes, anticipation of something potentially unpleasant is often more unpleasant than the event itself. Job interviews are no exception. With some solid effort and planning, you should be able to position yourself to get the best possible chance – and a chance is all any of us can expect when trying to land a job – for success.

Doing Your Homework

Say someone calls you and asks if you'll be free later that week for a phone interview. (This is the most common first step a company takes before inviting someone in for a face-to-face discussion. It helps them weed out potentially unfit candidates without wasting a hiring manager's time or the candidate's if the fit isn't right.) You quickly set a time and date for the call, make sure to get the name of the person you'll be speaking with, and tell them you're looking forward to the experience.

Your preparation should start the minute you hang up the phone. Quickly write down everything the person mentioned. Will the caller be interviewing you, will it be someone from HR, or will the hiring manager be the person on the other end of the line? Did the person drop anything in what he or she said about the position and what the company's looking for? How did he or she sound, positive and energetic

or tired and frustrated?

Once you've done this, it's time to go to work. In your

parents' day, researching a company meant going to the library

and looking up the company's history, checking its annual

reports, seeing if any articles had been published about the

firm, and other printed information. In the electronic age, most

if not all of this is readily available at your fingertips, which is

why *it's inexcusable not to spend a lot of time on the*

company's Web site. "It astounds me how many people

interview with companies without knowing anything about

what they do, what their mission is, or what working for them

is like," says one recruiter. "Coming in and telling us you're

interested in working for us because you need a job and we

have one may be true, but if you can't answer a few basic

questions about who we are, what we do, and why you want to

work for us, you haven't really positioned yourself for success."

A quick glance at the Web site can tell you a lot right away – such as whether the company is conservative or creative in its outlook, developed in its business practices or still a start-up operation, and countless other details. If the firm is an established one with a strong corporate history, take some time and download the annual report. (Yes, it's admittedly going to be very dry reading, but nothing else will tell you more about the company's operations and finances than its annual report to shareholders; even if you're not looking to go into a financial position, this is still worthwhile.) Thinking about interviewing with a nonprofit? Their annual report may not include the same level of financial data, but it will give you insight into the company's values, its mission and outlook, as well as the people who work for it.

Planning to interview for a smaller firm or a start-up company? The Web site will still contain some valuable information you want to make sure to review. Look at the Web site the way the employer is going to look at *you*. Remember, this is a two-way street – just as you want them to see if you're a good fit for their organization, so you want to see if they would be a good fit for you as well. Does the Web site contain dropped links and spelling errors? Is the phone contact information valid or has the line been disconnected? These kinds of things can give you a quick snapshot of the company and its level of organization. Keep a critical eye as you click through the pages so you have a solid idea of what you're in for if you go to work for this particular organization. Don't be afraid to be critical; just because you notice a mistake doesn't mean that the company is bad or that they don't necessarily appreciate precision; however, if this is your first exposure to the firm, first impressions should count just the same for them as for you.

Next Steps

Okay, you've looked at the company's Web site and gotten to know a little bit about how it operates. What next?

To really excel, you need to be ready to go above and beyond what other applicants are going to do. Most will give the Web site a quick review and make some notes before proceeding with the interview, so this is your chance to really dig down deep. What about the company is *not* covered on its Web site? How can you find this out?

This is where your networking skills come into play. Is there someone in your network who currently works or who has worked for the firm? Can he or she tell you about what it's like to work there, both in terms of the good and the bad? (Side note: Be very wary of anyone who tells you, "There is no bad to working here." Every place has its ups and downs; and anyone who can't be honest with you isn't someone you want to work with.) Can they put you in touch with anyone else who can tell you about the company and what their experiences working there have been? Tap your contacts and see if anyone knows anyone who has worked at the firm and then reach out to them for the inside scoop. (Yes, you will need to park any shyness at the door here; but here's the secret when reaching out to find out more about a job: *Everyone* has been where you are and probably remembers the difficulties job seekers face, so more often than not you will probably find people you don't know are willing to spare a few moments to share some information with you if you know how to ask.)

Once you've completed this, keep going. Has anyone in your online social network worked at the firm before? How about your school alumni office? Do any of your past job contacts know anyone who used to work at this firm? Chances are with a minimal amount of digging, you can find at least a few people who once worked at the place or who know someone who has and who would be more than happy to spend a few minutes telling you the ins and outs of the company and its culture.

Do many of these people include the company on their online profiles? If so, take a closer look. Did most of them spend a great deal of time there, or did most of them leave after only a few months or a year? A high rate of turnover should be a clear sign that people who worked there were either unfulfilled, unhappy, or quickly burned out. Don't be afraid to ask about this when you talk to them, and don't think of this as being rude. If you're going to be going to work at the place, you want to know as much as possible before starting there. If someone tells you on one hand that he enjoyed the place and found it a lot of fun but on the other hand only stayed there six months, you're perfectly within your rights to ask why if it was so wonderful he left after such a short period of time.

Remember, you're not trying to trip the person up but trying to

get a full picture of what it is like working at this particular

place.

Fine, you say, but what kinds of questions should you

ask? And how should you go about reaching out to someone

you don't even know to ask what sound like very personal

questions? Again, think proactively – your purpose is not just

to get information from this person but also to *establish a*

connection. Can this person be part of your network? Is there

something you can do for him or her in exchange for this

information? Can you meet them for coffee or lunch

somewhere in return for their information? Keeping the two-

way street in mind will go a long way toward opening up

opportunities with someone for communicating.

Some good things to think about asking include:

- How would you describe your experiences at the company? What was it like working there?

- What can you tell me about the interview process? (Is it behavioral, case, panel, etc.) How many interviews will I go through before hearing back?

- Was there an onboarding process to help you get acquainted with the company and its people? If so, what was it like?

- Whom did you report to while you were there? What was it like working for him or her? Did this person know the person I'll be interviewing with? Did you?

- What were the hours like? Was the overtime expected and constant or was it cyclical and something you could plan for?

- What were the performance reviews like?

- Why did you leave the company? Would you go back there if another position opened up?

- What would you say were the best things about working there? What were the worst?

- What would you tell someone thinking about working there?

- *Is there anything I can do for you while we are networking?*

If you're able to establish even just one or two connections who worked at the firm through your network or contacts, you're in a great position to compare notes from the people you speak with and the person you'll be talking to. If your sources' notes pretty much align with each other, you probably have a pretty good indication of what it's like to work at the firm. On the other hand, if what your sources tell you and what the screening interviewer tells you differ strongly, consider it a warning sign. People who no longer work at a company are usually in a much better position to speak frankly and honestly about their experiences vs. someone who is still with the firm and looking to fill a position. Take anything you hear with a grain of salt – ex-employees could have axes to grind against a firm for any number of reasons – but generally the person on the outside has less reason to lie than someone on the inside who is desperately trying to fill a position.

Become a Collector

Once you've reviewed the Web site and talked with people, it's time to put together your briefing folder. This is where you'll put every piece of information you collect about a company, from contact testimonials to press releases and printouts. Your goal is to develop as detailed a profile of the firm as possible so you know as much as you can about it before going into any interviews.

Some things to look up and include:

- Press releases and articles about the firm

- Annual and quarterly reports, 10-K and 8-K filings

- Staff and officer profiles

- Sample reports and documents compiled by the company

- Business Web site profiles

- Potential competitors

- Information about the market or industry of the firm (trends, economic developments, recent innovations, etc.)

- Any e-mails or contact information, particularly those that include addresses and phone numbers

Before you start pounding your head against the wall over all this effort, remember that your objective is *not* to memorize this information so much as it is to be readily familiar with it in order to develop a good sense of how the company operates, what its culture is like, and whether you would be a good fit for the organization. It also goes a long way toward helping you prepare for the inevitable questions you will be asked during the interview. Being asked, "So, what do you know about us?" and only being able to repeat a few bits from the Web site may get you a polite nod, but being able to speak quickly and thoroughly about the company and its history, its achievements, and some recent market developments that you could help with will put you in a class by yourself, particularly if all your peers did was check the Web site the morning of their interview.

Becoming a Scriptwriter

Once you've complied your information folder and familiarized yourself with the company and its operations, it's time to begin writing your interview script. Most phone screenings and face-to-face interviews involve standard sets of questions with one or two variants thrown in for good measure. Some of the most common questions include:

- Tell me a little about yourself.

- Tell me what you know about our firm.

- How did you hear about us? How did you learn about this opening?

- Why do you want to come and work for us?

- I noticed on your resume that you did _____. What can you tell me about that?

- How much experience do you have with _____?

- Why did you leave your last job? (*If you had another job before this one.*)

- How would you describe your work style?

- What would you say is your greatest strength? How about your greatest weakness? (Yes, this one is tiresome but still gets asked.)

- Where do you see yourself in 3-5 years? (*Do not mention any plans for graduate school here or you'll be seen as a short-timer who won't be with the firm for very long.*)

- Tell me about a challenge you recently encountered at work and how you overcame it.

- Tell me about a time you were on a team and had a problem with someone. How did you handle it?

This is where your research should begin to pay off. As you prepare some scripted responses to the questions, keep in mind any special priorities you came across during your research. Does the company place a great deal of value on teams? This would be a good time to mention the recycling committee you chaired in school or the charity drive you organized as part of a fraternity project. Does the company's mission statement include any buzzwords or phrases you can find a way to slip into your responses without repeating them verbatim? If so, find some spots where the wording might fit in one or two of your answers.

Overall, your goal should be to try and come up with between three and five (no more) bullet points for each question you expect to be asked. For each, practice saying aloud how you would respond to the question, making sure not to rush through your answer. (You will always talk more quickly during the interview due to stress, so make sure to speak slowly during your practice sessions so any speeding up will be relative.) Take several minutes to look over your resume and plan what you will say about each bullet and position that you listed. As with the expected questions, you'll want to have a short (no more than 90 seconds) anecdote or story to relate with each one.

For each answer, you'll want to cover the basics:

- What happened (what was the challenge you faced, the obstacle you needed to overcome, the goal you wanted to reach, etc.)?

- What did you do (what steps you took to resolve the situation, which people you spoke with, how you went about attacking the problem, etc.)?

- What was the result (if it was bad, you need a different example)?

Of each step, the most important is the one at the end where you tie the story together. What did you and your group learn from the experience you are describing? What did you conclude based on what you went through? What was your take-away from the assignment or challenge? These are the things your interviewer will be looking for, and your goal is to guide him or her to this carefully crafted conclusion that convinces him or her that you're the right person for the job.

Many people – particularly those who have been in the workforce for an extended period – make the mistake of thinking they need to be overly thorough with job interview answers. Asking them to tell a "little" about themselves means having to sit through an endless recapitulation of every war story the person has lived through, who they worked with, what their accomplishments were, etc. *Never fall into this trap.* Your goal is to have a good, short story with a positive conclusion that wraps up your example for the interviewer. Droning on and on for the purposes of thoroughness without getting to the point not only wastes valuable time, but it also does little to help your chances of landing the job.

Compare the following responses:

Interviewer 1: So, Ms. Johnson, tell me a little about yourself

Ms. Johnson: Well, I was senior consultant for ABC

Consultants, where I worked for five years under Jack Jobholder. Before that, I was associate consultant for XYZ consultants in Atlanta, where I handled all of our banking client accounts. Before that, I worked at Employee Dynamics firm, where I was in charge of all our east side clients. These would be the people who were responsible for 50% of our business. I was there for about two years, and before that I worked briefly with Hiring People, Inc. I did that for only about a year before I left to go to work for Generic Company, Inc. Before that...

Interviewer 1: (Wants to crawl inside her desk and die...)

Interviewer 2: So, Ms. Waxman, tell me a little about yourself.

Ms. Waxman: Well, I was working for ABC Consultants for the past three years. I've handled several of our major accounts, which is why I think this would be a great opportunity for me here since I understand your company has a very similar client base. I'm very familiar with our industry, not just because of my work at ABC but also the work I did at my earlier company, XYZ consultants. At both firms, I was able to reduce our expenses by nearly ten percent through re-engineering and competitive estimating. I think these put me in a great position for this assignment, because I understand you're looking to reduce expenses as well given the tight market conditions that we're all facing right now.

Notice the different responses. The first candidate went off on an endless summary of her work experiences for different companies – most of which are already outlined on her resume – without giving the interviewer anything of real value or explaining how her experiences prepared her to work for the interviewer's firm. Assuming she's even still listening, the interviewer's impression is probably tending more toward the negative than positive at this stage, and the candidate's battle more than likely will be uphill from here on out. The second candidate, however, kept her pitch to the job at hand, summarizing only how her most recent experiences were relevant to the job and what she could bring to the table. She demonstrated strong knowledge of the industry and market in which the company operates, and she kept her answer brief and to the point.

Now, ask yourself this question: Which candidate would *you* be most likely to hire?

Fielding Curves

Fine, you say to yourself. This is all well and good, but what about the questions I *haven't prepared for*? What about the queries that come out of left field that I never could have prepared for because there was simply no way I could have seen them coming? How do I handle that?

Many public-relations and graduate communication courses, teach a very simple rule: *Always have your main talking points, and always stick to them.* When asked something unrelated that you could not have prepared for, the worst thing you can do is allow yourself to be led astray and follow the interviewer down the proverbial rabbit hole. Instead, remember your main lines of focus and bullet points you're prepared to speak to, circle back to them, and stay there.

Admittedly, this is easier said than done. If you're asked, "If you were a tree, what kind of tree would you be and why?" it may be difficult to take the question seriously, but don't let it show. Instead, think back to your experiences and prepared responses, and see what you can draw from them. For instance, most people probably say something like, "I'd be a Redwood or an oak – something strong and sturdy." This is nice, but it doesn't give the interviewer a whole lot to go with. Instead, try something that ties into your experiences and provides you with a platform for discussing how your qualifications meet the position. "That's a good question," you say, pausing to compose your answer. "I guess whichever tree I was, it would have to be something that is flexible and can move with the winds, because that's what I've always had to do at my job. If something came up, I had to be willing to move to make it happen. For example, during my last job, we had a situation…"

If this sounds cheesy, bear in mind that a certain amount of being able to handle strange and unusual experiences – as well as the cheesy – goes with any job. If that's not enough to convince you, consider this: If you ask *any* job seeker what was the most ridiculous or unusual question he or she has ever been asked, chances are they all have come across something along these lines – if not worse – at one time or another. Expect to field a few strange ground balls from time to time; but always remember your main talking points. These are the experiences, skills, and knowledge areas you want to drive home to the interviewer, so any outside-the-circle questions, while understandable, should still give you some opportunity to work your way back to your main points.

Illegal Questions

While most firms will not willingly or intentionally ask you questions that they know to be illegal, chances are you may find yourself at one time or another fielding a question that makes you uncomfortable or which raises a yellow caution light. For instance, while firms may not ask about protected issues like marital status or sexual orientation, they *may* ask questions designed to reveal areas of your background that would otherwise inhibit you performing your duties as required. Thus, while the company may not ask if you are married with small children, they *may* inquire whether you would have any difficulties meeting a demanding travel schedule that goes with a particular position. People with small children and families who don't like to be away from them for extended periods of time will usually respond that they have family commitments and do not want to be separated from their wives/husbands/children for weeks or months at a time. A quick search of the Internet can usually help you come up with a listing of what kinds of questions are permitted and which are not, but most employers will try to steer clear of marital situations, family plans, ethnicity and sexual orientation, and similar areas.

Nevertheless, such questions may still come up. If you are asked a question that you know to be illegal, take a few moments to decide whether you really want to answer it. Although it is always possible the interviewer is unaware that he or she is breaking the law by asking an inappropriate question, the fact that the question has been put to you reveals

a great deal about the level of organization at the company.
Put more simply, there are really three possibilities why you've
been asked something illegal or inappropriate: the company has
no HR department (and thus there is no one to advise the
interviewer on what topics can and cannot be addressed), HR
did not properly advise the interviewer as to what kinds of
questions are legal and illegal, or – in the worst case – the
interviewer is knowingly disregarding HR's advice. In every
instance, these should be considered warning signs about the
level of organization and the ethics of the company.
Admittedly, refusing to answer the question or pointing out
how and why it is illegal may diminish your chances with the
firm, but it may also save you unfathomable headaches down
the line if you decide to go to work for the company despite
this warning sign and later find out it was symptomatic of the
(lack of) ethics at the organization.

Fine, you say, but how do I answer the question? You have two choices: You can either answer the question or be direct, "I'm sorry, but I don't think that's an appropriate question," can be the best and most sincere way of addressing something head-on. It may admittedly damn your chances of hiring, but it is also entirely possible that the interviewer asked the question intentionally to see how you would react. In the end, there's not so much a "right" path to follow in these instances as much as there is simply the chance to go with your gut and trust if something does not feel right. Remember, *your goal is never to find a job, it's to find the job that is right for you.*

The Phone Screening

Once you've completed your script and your research for the company, you should be all set for any preliminary telephone screenings the company wishes to put you through as part of that first step. Most screenings can last anywhere from 15-20 minutes to as long as 40-45 minutes. They are not likely to go beyond this if for no other reason than because the interviewer likely has several calls to make and needs to allow enough time to get through them and make a recommendation as to which candidates were suitable for the next round of interviews. (And interviewers get tired of asking the same questions just as you get tired of answering them...)

Treat the interview like a face to face conversation. You want to respond *slowly and clearly* to all the questions the interviewer asks, drawing particular attention to the areas you noted where your qualifications meet the needs for the position. Be polite and cheerful, but avoid the temptation to crack jokes or make sarcastic asides. Remember, as with e-mail and text messages, context is everything, and without the ability to insert an emoticon or read a facial expression, the person on the other end of the line could mistakenly come away with a very different impression than the one you intend simply because they can't see your face during the conversation.

Also, be in tune to the interviewer's day and schedule: If it's Monday and you're the last call of the day, chances are the person is going to be tired and hoping to wind things down quickly. On the other hand, if your interview is scheduled for a Friday morning and you sense the person on the other end of the line is in a good mood, don't be afraid to take a friendlier approach in your conversation style.

In addition to responding to the interviewer's questions, be prepared at the end of the conversation to ask some questions of your own about the position and about the person who is interviewing you. (A more detailed set of questions to ask during a face-to-face interview will be covered later in this chapter.) Ask about the basics of the job, what the company is looking for in its candidates, and how your skills fit the position. One excellent way of turning the tables on the interviewer without seeming disruptive would be to ask the interviewer what qualifications the company is looking for, and then ask which of your qualifications they think would best match the position. By doing this, you've essentially "jujitsued" the interviewer into highlighting why you would be a good fit for the position. (This also gives you ammunition for any follow up face-to-face interviews with other people since you can now mention how this interviewer spoke regarding your qualifications and how they matched the position.)

Additionally, don't be afraid to ask the interviewer about his or her background. What made them decide to come to work for the company, and how long have they been with the firm? (Don't be surprised if you hear, "Oh, well, it was a job, so…" This is actually a far more common answer than you might think, but it is still one *you* should avoid giving during your part of the interview.) Pay close attention to what the interviewer tells you, particularly his or her tone, attitude, and feelings about the company. Someone who is happy to work at a particular firm will probably gush about how wonderful it is, what the people are like, and will likely have been there for an extended period of time. On the other hand, someone who is just going through the motions of asking questions on a prepared list and filling in your responses may still like the job, but telling the difference between them should not be difficult.

Last but not least, make sure you've selected some times that would work for a follow-up interview in case they ask for one. This is not to be presumptuous on your part, but rather to make sure you come across as prepared and organized to your interviewer. Telling them right away that you have time on "Thursday or Friday between 2:00 and 4:00" vs. saying, "I'm not sure what my schedule is, let me get back to you..." obviously makes much stronger impression. If the interviewer wants to push things back to the following week, make sure you know which dates and times will work for you then as well, especially if you are already employed at another job and will need to arrange for time off to have the interview.

A final word on questions: Beware of any company that does not allow you time for asking questions of your own during a phone screen or face to face interview. If they are not interested in answering your questions, they likely have something to hide, have already selected the candidate they wish to hire, or have very poor management. If the latter is the case, you probably do not want to be working there in the first place.

Dry Runs

Okay, suppose you have passed the phone interview and landed a follow-up. What's next?

Since your goal is to always leave as little as possible to chance, your next step is to go out and actually *do a dry run getting to and from the company for your interview*. If possible, you want to do it close to the actual time of your interview so you can gauge what the traffic conditions will be like and learn how much time will be required to get to the location. If you will be coming from work and taking a taxi or riding the subway, make notes of the time it takes getting to the company and back to your office or home and then add 20 or 30 minutes as a cushion. You can always make a note of any coffee shops, convenience stores, or restaurants nearby where you can collect your thoughts or review any last-minute notes if you find yourself early with some extra time. Finding yourself lost on the way to the interview or missing a critical turn that you could have learned on an earlier practice run only serves to add further stress to an already tense situation, which is something you definitely want to avoid.

The other reason to do a dry run is that it gives you an opportunity to scope out the company's location and surrounding areas. Is the building located in a safe part of town, or is it someplace you'd rather not be after dark? Is there a parking garage nearby that's reasonably priced or a subway station that is easily accessible? (Bear in mind you will need to deduct transportation and parking from whatever salary you earn.) What are the nearby coffee shops, restaurants, and businesses like? Do they seem clean and inviting, or is there graffiti on the walls and bars on the windows? Are the nearby shopping areas busy and well-lit, or are they vacant and run-down? If you have the time, make a point of stopping in a few of the places and seeing what they are like. A few minutes talking with a proprietor of a store may tell you more than anything else you see about what the neighborhood is like and what kinds of people work and live there. Remember, it's not just about the company that you want to see, it's as much about getting to and from it that will make a difference for you over time. Finding the best job that's a long haul from home may not seem too bad at first, but several weeks or months into the job, those stressful commutes will start to take their toll.

Look for Brown M&Ms

Okay, the big day is here. After doing all your research and rehearsal, your dry run and your scouting, you're ready to take on the interview. What should you look to do and what should you do once you arrive?

First, make sure before leaving that you have what you'll need. A good checklist includes:

- Directions to the office
- Extra copies of your resume (at least two or three)
- Notes regarding the name(s) of the person(s) you'll be meeting with
- A copy of the job description

- Your notes folder

Most job experts recommend aiming to arrive at least 10 to 15 minutes before your interview. Twenty might seem like overkill and catch your interviewer off guard, so even if you do wind up earlier than expected because of light traffic or unexpected good fortune, put the time to good use and scout around. You can also look for indicators that can tell you more about the company in just a few moments than all your research up to this point:

- Is the inside of the office clean and neat, or are there boxes stacked up in the halls?

- Is the carpet new or worn? Are the walls clean or scuffed? Is there wiring hanging out of areas where ceiling panels have been removed?

- Does the person at the front desk greet you pleasantly or in a surly tone? Bear in mind that front office personnel are usually mirrors for their supervisors since people always prefer to hire those like themselves. If you're greeted in a friendly manner, consider it a positive sign. If not or the person meeting you is rude, don't write off the experience altogether, but make a note of it. First impressions are a two-way street.

- How are the people entering and leaving dressed? Are they dressed casually, professionally, or in jeans and sneakers? Are they laughing and smiling or is everyone speaking in a hushed tone and moving quickly toward the exit so as not to be overheard?

After making your mental notes, talk to the security guard or receptionist and tell them your name and who you're there to see. The other person will tell you to have a seat. Before doing so, smile back and ask, "Is there a restroom I could use?"

134

But what if I don't have to use the restroom? Go anyway. The restroom, like the proverbial brown M&M™ candies, is a microcosm of information about the company and its practices (see box).

The Power of M&Ms as a Safety Indicator

Years ago, the hard-rock rock band Van Halen was infamously rumored to have had a clause put into its contracts that required their dressing rooms to be furnished with bowl of M&M™ candies *with all the brown ones removed*.

Sounds like an urban legend, right? Arrogant rock stars at their worst doing something ridiculous just because they can? As it turned out, the band *did* have such a rider in its contracts, but the rider was there for a very specific purpose: to make sure promoters had read the contract and noted its safety provisions and stage support requirements. In other words, the M&M™ requirement was like the proverbial canary-in-the-coal-mine; it told the band at a glance whether their contract had been read and followed or whether it had been ignored.

If the band showed up and the M&M™ refreshment bowl was clear of brown candies, they knew their road crew could do a cursory check of the stage setup before the show and that things would likely be fine. If, however, they arrived to see brown M&M™ candies in the bowl, it was an instant signal that the contract had not been read in detail. That, in turn, was a red flag, because it meant that important safety precautions had likely been ignored. These could include any number of issues such as cables and wiring, pyrotechnic setups, load-bearing support structures, etc. Locating and fixing potential issues would cost time and money, so the band added the clause as a way of checking whether their instructions had been followed. They also got the benefit of additional publicity for the provision as well.

Much like the M&M™s, a company's restroom can tell you a great deal about it at a glance. Is it clean, or are there newspapers littering the floor? Are the soap dispensers full or empty? Is the trash bin overflowing with used paper towels? For that matter, *are* there paper towels? Do the stalls have toilet paper? Are the toilets clean or do they resemble an out-of-order stall at the local airport?

In terms of why this is important, stop and ask yourself this basic question: If a company is not able to keep its restrooms clean and stocked – and if a visitor's first glance is a filthy restroom that clearly is not being maintained – what impression does that give a first-time visitor or potential employee, and what does it say about the level of organization at the firm? Imagine you need to order supplies or submit a requisition for something business-related; which organization would you expect to be capable of processing the request expeditiously: the one with spotless restrooms that conveys a professional appearance, or the one that stinks and has no soap or paper towels? Again, this is by no means a *guarantee* of anything, but since you have only a limited amount of time to develop an impression – and since the company will be sizing you up at first sight as well – you should make all the mental notes you can based on what you see initially. Be wary of any place that fails the "restroom test."

The Meet and Greet

Your interviewer arrives. Rising from your chair, you shake the person's hand firmly (but not crushingly) and follow her back to the conference room for your interview. Chances are she'll ask you whether you had difficulty finding the place or would like a bottled water. While this may seem like a nice gesture, remember that *no one wants to wait on someone else.* Politely decline the offer or, better still, bring your own bottle in case your throat gets dry.

After having a seat, the interviewer may ask a few more small talk questions to get you to relax before launching into the interview itself. You'll probably still feel some jitters, but hopefully your scripting and rehearsals have prepared you up to this point. Nevertheless, there are still some things to try and remember:

- **Don't talk too quickly.** Polished public speakers always know that when they're on stage delivering their speeches, things happen more quickly. You're nervous, you're energized, the adrenaline is flowing, and you find yourself racing through your words or flying through your lines. Make a point of *pausing* before each answer to collect your thoughts (or at least give the appearance of collecting them even if you know what you're going to say). If nothing else, this will help you look contemplative in addition to helping you slow your speech.

- **Listen before responding.** Many candidates make the mistake of launching into their qualifications before fully understanding the question or getting a fuller picture of what they are being asked. If all you are doing is telling them why you're so good instead of listening to what it is they specifically need, you may be hurting yourself rather than helping. Listen carefully to what is being said and asked, and then check for certainty before answering.

- **Don't fidget.** It's human nature when nervous to want to move – we tap our feet, flick our fingers, pick at a something, or do any number of things. *Don't do this.* Not only does it make you look nervous, but it distracts the interviewer and may also undermine your demeanor. Always remember, most communication is nonverbal, so if your words are well-chosen and calmly expressed but your right foot is tapping incessantly, guess which is going to come across more convincingly to the interviewer?

- **Don't be too casual.** It is possible to overdo the calming approach and wind up going to the opposite extreme: Rather than coming across as nervous and fidgety, you instead project an almost lazy or careless attitude as you sink back into the overstuffed chair and cast your gaze out the window before answering. Make a point of sitting up straight and keeping your focus on the interviewer.

- **Don't take notes.** While it's perfectly understandable to want to record everything you discuss, learn to rely on making mental notes of any big issues or areas that come up during your conversation. Don't try to remember everything that you review, but make points of noting items of interest that you do cover.

- **Express interest in the job and company.** Sounds obvious, doesn't it? Not really. Most interviewees are usually so focused on answering the right questions that they forget their main goal is to seem excited and interested in the position. Does the job offer you a chance to do something you love? Will it be a kickstart toward that rewarding career you always wanted? Show some enthusiasm, but don't give in to being a cheerleader. Your goal is to make sure the interviewer knows you really want the position and would be happy to have it, not to come across as the poster child for Cheerleader U.

The Do's

As the interview begins, the interviewer will likely start by giving you an overview of the position and the company, telling you what will be expected of the person in the role and what he or she will be responsible for handling. It's perfectly natural to want to interrupt when something comes over that fits your skills, but hold your fire until the interviewer is ready to hear what you have to say.

After some cautious back and forth, the interviewer will likely ask if you have any questions for him or her. This is where all your preparation should start paying off in spades. Your questions should be detailed and, when necessary, direct and straightforward. By checking the Web site and talking to people ahead of time, you've hopefully been able to get the answers to most of your basic questions, so be sure to use this time to your advantage to get a more detailed feel for the position. (Asking something that is available on the Web site is a sure sign you did not do your homework and can be the kiss of death in an interview.) Some of your questions might include:

- *"Is this a new position (i.e., one that the company is creating based on a new need or set of needs) or a new vacancy?"* You'll want to ask this because you deserve to know how the opening came about. Did someone resign or quit? Get promoted? Leave the country under questionable circumstances? Make a point to learn this in detail.

- *"If this is a new vacancy, why did the last person leave this job?"* (Pay very close attention to the interviewer's words and body language here – if the departure was a difficult one for the people involved, there will likely be some shifting and breaking of eye contact, perhaps some stammering or evasive language, etc. Watch for this and make a note of exactly what you are told. Remember, you are interviewing the company as much as the company is interviewing you to make sure that there is a good fit for you both.

- *"How long was the last person in this job?"* If the position is entry-level, most people probably won't expect you to stay more than a year or two before moving on or up to something else. Still, if someone is in a position less than six months and leaves for anything other than a promotion, be cautious.

- *"What kind of advancement opportunities does this position create?"* Job experts go back and forth on the good and bad of asking this sort of question, but if this really is one of your first jobs out of undergrad – or your first one that does not involve waiting tables – you deserve to know what it will lead to or what skills you will develop while working there. You also signal by asking it that you are looking to stay with a firm rather than just have a job. A position that does not have this potential or which people come and go without ever really changing means you will likely have 6-12 months before you become bored and begin the search all over again as well. While this may be good insofar as getting you out from under your parents' roof, think carefully if it will offer you the stepping stone you want for a career.

- *"Who will I be working for? Can I meet some of the other people in the office I will be working with?"* Remember, although it is likely that the person interviewing you will be your boss, this is not always the case. Maybe HR wants a crack at you first, or maybe a higher-up restricts all the hiring decisions for himself or herself. Get to know your prospective boss and your team. (And *run as fast as you can in the other direction* if the company balks at letting you speak with anyone else on the team…)

- *"What types of skills are you looking for this new person to have that the previous person did not?"* This is your chance to highlight any skills you have that the interviewer mentions are considered essential for the position.

- *"How soon are you looking to get someone onboard?"* Most companies will understand if you need to give a two-week notice for another job, but it never hurts to ask for three both to give you extra time to tie up loose ends and take a few days off in between before starting something new. The company will look at this as a hopeful sign that you will show them the same courtesy in return if and when you ever decide to leave them as well.

- *"What are the benefits of this position and its challenges?"* What will be the pluses and the minuses? You deserve to know the good and the bad without necessarily bringing up the word *bad* in the discussion. Pay close attention to what is said and watch for any particular phrases that give you pause. If you're told, "We have had a hard time finding the right person for this position," keep in mind the issue is just as likely (if not more) to be the *company's* failure to define the position or organize its management appropriately as it is to have had a run of bad luck with candidates.

- *"Why did you decide this was where you wanted to work?"* Go ahead – ask! See what the interviewer has to say about whether it was just a job or if it's the people or something else entirely.

Above all, *pay attention to the energy dynamics in the interviewer's demeanor and questions.* Is she eagerly trying to find out more about you, or does she come across as simply someone going through the motions for the umpteenth time? Is she positive and helpful in answering your questions, or does she seem evasive in her responses? Do her answers seem genuine, or are they canned with too many business clichés? Don't be afraid to probe a bit deeper to some responses. Finding out someone "empowers" employees could mean anything from giving them free reign to ignoring them completely until there's a crisis and it's time to blame someone. Similarly, someone who "runs a tight ship" could be someone who insists on weekly meetings and updates (good) or who believes in micromanaging every little detail and controlling not only what you do but how you do it (bad). And if someone says, "We need someone who can hit the ground

149

running…" it likely means they want someone who already has the requisite skills and will not require any formal training.

As always, learn to trust your gut, and don't be afraid to probe if something strikes you as amiss.

The Don'ts

Just as there are many things to remember to do during the interview, there are also a number of things you should remember *not* to do as well. While it's nearly always better to be honest with the interviewer, it is also possible to be too honest and inadvertently doom your chances for the position. Here are some common pitfalls to avoid:

- **Don't criticize your last job or boss.** Sure, your last boss may have been a tyrant or an evil witch who reveled in nothing more than making your life miserable, but *under no circumstances should you mention this*. Resist the temptation to rehash things if they will result in your trashing former bosses or coworkers or if you know bringing them up will stir bad memories. Your goal is to appear above that sort of thing, even if deep down inside everyone knows that at one time or another everybody winds up working for someone they can't stand or who made life insufferable for those around them. Suck it up and take the high road.

- **Don't mention any future plans to attend graduate school.** Even if the interviewer himself mentions plans to attend UNC next fall, don't say you're looking to do the same thing in a couple of years. Telling a prospective employer that you're planning to attend grad school raises all kinds of cautionary flags, not just in terms of your long-term temporary status ("Oh, great. If we hire him, he'll only be with us for a year or two...") but also in terms of your expected work ethic ("After 18 months, his commitment will start to sag as he gears up for school..."). If your plans do include attending grad school in the future, say that you've looked into it and wouldn't rule it out but that your main focus right now is on this position and moving your career forward.

- **Be careful addressing any shortcomings.** No one expects you to fully disclose every mistake you ever made, but know in advance how you will address any gaps in your resume or any potential disruptions in your work history. Try to find a positive spin for any negative experiences that you can point to in terms of a learning experience and keep the focus there. Telling the interviewer that you had to leave a particular job "for personal reasons" and that your next position "was a much better fit, because it

allowed better use of my skills in these areas…"
will go over a lot better than saying, "I was fired."

- **Be careful asking about salary and benefits.**
  There are admittedly different schools of thought here, but ideally you should have some idea of this before you go in for the interview. Nobody wants to waste valuable time screening candidates only to select one at the end and discover that they are worlds apart in terms of salary. If you are asked about your expectations, feel free to answer with a range, but *avoid giving a specific figure* since you want to leave some wiggle room. A specific figure runs the risk of landing you either as someone asking for too much or someone willing to work for chump change; neither of which you want to be. Additionally, keep in mind that a job paying more than your last salary may seem fantastic at first

glance, but if you find six months into the gig that you were hired well below what your predecessor was earning – and that it is far below what others at the firm with comparable experience are making – will quickly turn your feelings of triumph and satisfaction to anger and resentment.

- **If you already have a job and are looking for a new one, do not give the green light to talk to your present employer unless there's an offer.** A lot of firms ask this on their questionnaires, but the question is pretty much a lose-lose for you as a candidate. Telling prospective employers that they can't contact your current one sends a questionable signal ("Is this person hiding something?") while saying yes invites them to let the cat out of the bag that you're looking for a new job. The best way to handle this is to be confident and say, "I'd be happy to have you talk with my current / recent supervisor; but for obvious reasons I'd like to hold off on that until we reach an offer stage." The interviewer and firm should respect this answer; but if they don't or disregard your wishes and call your employer before extending an offer, consider this a breach of good faith and a sign that the employer cannot be trusted. Remember, no matter how badly you may want to leave a place or land a job, going to work for another firm that you know you can't trust is only likely to extend your job search in the long run since you will in all likelihood find yourself searching again when things turn sour.

Following Up

After the interview, the interviewer will likely walk you back to the front office or elevator, thanking you for your time and your interest in the firm. Remind the interviewer why you want the job and why you think the position would be a good fit and ask what the next steps might be. Ask for her business card so you can be sure to have a way of contacting her in the next few weeks should your schedule change or should you need to follow up on any next steps. (You'll also want to make sure you have an accurate spelling of her name when sending any e-mails.)

Once you're out the door and out of sight, reach into your briefcase and pull out your job folder. Write down everything that you remember discussing, particularly any strong points or negative ones that came up. Was there a question you were asked that you weren't prepared for or that slipped through your research? Write it down for future reference. Did you find yourself tripped up in your answer to anything? Make a note for the next time. Chances are if you rehearsed everything carefully, any minor slips will only be noticed by you vs. the interviewer, but if at some point you found yourself floundering or grasping for words, consider this a sign of something you need to address. Make special notes of anything you will want to check or confirm later, particularly if anything you heard conflicted with what you were told or uncovered in your research. Don't try to be too thorough at this stage; your only goal is to make note of things you might forget later.

That evening, take some time to unwind or relax before beginning any follow-up steps. If you weren't able to go for a run that morning, go for a light jog or quick swim to clear your head. If you have a favorite hobby, such as playing guitar or yoga, reward yourself with some well-earned recreation. You may even find while doing another activity that your mind suddenly snaps to something that happened in the interview that you'll want to note or ask about in the future.

After dinner, sit down and go over your notes from the interview. If you are inclined, go ahead and make a pro-con-Q list of all the things you've learned (pros for the good, cons for the bad, and Qs for any questions that you still have or which would affect your decisions). Think back not just over what you discussed but also about what you saw at the company and what impressions it gave you. If you were interviewing with a large consulting firm and came away impressed, put a check in the "pro" column. On the other hand, if you interviewed at a field office for a large firm and saw nothing but a dilapidated cubicle farm with several mouse traps under people's desks, make a note for your "con" column. Then, fire up your computer and pull out that business card so you can draft a short and breezy thank-you to the interviewer.

You'll want to cover just the quick basics:

- Thank her for her time and for giving you a chance to learn more about the position

- Highlight how your background and skills fit the position, preferably mentioning two or three examples (but not more)

- Mention you'll be looking forward to hearing from her again and taking any next steps

- Save the e-mail as a template for your next interview – you may even want to track which follow-ups tend to generate better responses just in case a particular combination of skills and wording seems to resonate more strongly with employers

After you've written the e-mail, save it and do something else. Get a drink of water and watch television. Play more guitar. After a half-hour or so, come back and re-read your message. Does it still sound okay? Cover everything it needs to cover? Good. You're almost set.

Why almost? Because at this point, you're just about ready to send the message, but you haven't taken the final step that most applicants forget about, namely, *running the spell-check on your message and proofing it carefully*. If you've gotten to this point and made a wonderful impression, the last thing you want to do is blow it by inadvertently inserting a typo or misspelling in your message. If you don't have a friend or roommate who can proof the message for you, force yourself to read *each word* slowly and out loud. You want to make sure nothing has been inadvertently omitted or left out. For instance, compare the following sample thank-you e-mails:

To: Irene Interviewer

From: Janet Jobapplicant

Hi, Irene,

Thanks for talking with me this afternoon about the editorial assistant position. I'm very glad we had chance to go over the position and its requirements.

I think my background in journalism, combined with my work on both the college newspaper and quarterly magazine, put me in an excellent position to bring my editorial expertise to Publications, Inc.

I'll look forward to our next steps, but if you or anyone else have any questions, please feel free contact me at janet.jobabpplicant@email.com.

Sincerely,

Janet Jobapplicant

Did you catch the errors? The e-mail was spelled correctly, but Janet made two critical omissions in her e-mail that – unless you were proofreading *very* carefully – were almost impossible to catch

    She started out well:

To: Irene Interviewer

From: Janet Jobapplicant

But then she went on and got careless:

Hi, Irene,

Thanks for talking with me this afternoon about the editorial assistant position. I'm very glad we had the chance to go over the position and its requirements.

I think my background in journalism, combined with my work on both the college newspaper and quarterly magazine, put me in an excellent position to bring my editorial expertise to Publications, Inc.

I'll look forward to our next steps, but if you or anyone else have any questions, please feel free to contact me at janet.jobabpplicant@email.com.

Sincerely,

Janet Jobapplicant

Such omissions are among the easiest errors to make when revising an e-mail for someone. (And if we wanted to nitpick even further, we could mention that Janet used the word "position" twice in two sentences instead of finding a synonym or changing her wording.) Even more problematic, however, is that the errors she made are not the kind spell-checkers normally catch. This is why, if you can't find someone to proof your e-mail for you, make sure you take a break from writing it so you can come back with a fresh pair of eyes and make a point of reading *every* word so you can make absolutely sure you do not overlook anything. The worst thing you can do after laying so much excellent groundwork is torpedo your chances with a careless mistake that could have been caught with a simple spell-check or read-through.

Ready? Take a deep breath and hit *send*.

Calendar Notes

After you've sent your e-mail and before you shut down your computer, go into whatever calendar program you use (or handwritten date book that you keep) and make a note in a week or two to follow up. You will want to wait at least a week so as not to seem overly anxious but not more than two since you want to make sure you're still fresh in her memory and on her radar screen. Include with the note any particular details about that day's interview and conversation so you can reference them in any follow-up correspondence. Did you two find you shared a hobby or personal interest? A love of the outdoors or skiing? Passion for the environment? Don't be afraid to include it in your follow up message.

If a couple of weeks go by without word, consider it a cautionary sign, but don't give up hope entirely. It's possible that the interviewer is still talking with candidates whose schedules required reworking to fit or has had to take some time off for personal needs. Maybe a crisis got dropped in her lap and required her to put everything on hold for several days before she could get back to screening candidates. Maybe her boss put a hold on the position until something else could be resolved. In short, there could be any number of reasons for a delay that have zero to do with you or your chances.

On the other hand, if after sending your follow-up e-mail a few weeks go by and you still hear nothing back, don't hesitate to drop a polite check-in message to keep in touch. If still more time passes, however, step back and reconsider. A decent (read: professional) organization will find time to follow up with you, even if all you get back is a form e-mail thanking you for your time and interest. A personalized response from the interviewer – even one that makes no mention of anything promising but which does reference some specific aspects of your background – is a better sign, but a lack of any response whatsoever means that the company is either not particularly interested or that people are overloaded and cannot find the time to respond. When you're on the track for selection, things will tend to happen quickly; if they don't, it's more often than not a sign that something else is brewing.

If you still decide that the position and the company are worth the effort, make another note to follow up in a week or two but no more. Tell the interviewer that you really enjoyed meeting with her and are still very interested in the position but that you do need an update so you can know whether the position is still open or if you need to be "considering other options." You don't need to be specific about the options you may be considering – particularly if there really aren't any at the moment – but if 3-4 weeks go by without reply of any kind, you may need to write the interview off as a learning experience and keep searching. The company may still come back at some point, but be wary – a professional outfit that is really interested in your skills will make a point of trying to get back to you as quickly as possible so as to make sure they don't lose a promising employee or at the very least to keep you posted. Those that don't or which don't care about their employees and consider one hire just as expendable as another may not be the best places to work.

Dealing with Rejection

Face it: Everyone gets hurt in the job search. Even with your best efforts, research, and rehearsal, more often than not something can – and often will – tip the scales in someone else's favor. Maybe the company decided to promote somebody from within at the last moment, or maybe another candidate just happened to have a particular set of skills "we didn't even know we needed until we saw them on his resume." Maybe a supervisor used his or her weight to get a responsibility changed to fit her department's needs in addition to the one you interviewed for. Or maybe the position was already filled but the firm felt compelled to go through the interview process to cover their bases. In short, there can literally be any number of reasons why something may or may not have worked out for you; the most difficult aspect of dealing with it is that in most cases you'll never really know the actual reasons behind the decision.

If you get a letter or an e-mail advising you that "another candidate's background better suits our needs," feel free to vent privately but under no circumstances fire anything back. Feeling angry is understandable, but bear in mind that interviews are the battle while getting a job is the war. Go for another jog or a swim, ride your bike, or hit the gym to get some exercise and push whatever anger you have out of your system as much as possible. You'll need to do this for your next step.

And what is that step? Probably the most difficult one of all. After finishing your exercise regimen and having a chance to calm yourself, sit down at the computer and compose a polite thank-you to the interviewer and the firm, telling them that while you're certainly disappointed to learn you won't be working there, you did appreciate the opportunity and enjoyed talking with the people you met. (And yes, save this as a template for future reference as well.)

Why humble yourself like this after getting kicked in the teeth? Because every once in a while – not often, but once in a while – things change after a candidate is hired. Maybe the person they bring on board has the requisite skills sets but can't get along with the rest of the people in the office. Maybe he accepts the position but gets another offer two weeks later that is closer to where he lives and pays more. Maybe after hiring him the company learns that some of the skills he listed on his resume were misleading or false. The point is, anything can change, so your goal is to appear as gracious as possible in defeat while still indicating an interest in the firm. In this way, your thinking is long-term, not short term; just because this one position did not work out does not mean future ones will not if and when they become available.

Along that same line of thought, what if the position *does* work out for this other person, but in six months he decides to try something else while you're still looking? What if he gets promoted or transferred? What if his position gets downgraded and he decides to quit? Again, any number of things can happen that could cause the company to reopen its search, so your goal should not only be to appear as magnanimous as possible but also to stay on the periphery so you can still have an opportunity should one come about.

How do you do this? Go back to the same methods you've learned. If you felt a strong connection to the interviewer, make a note on your calendar to drop him or her a line from time to time – perhaps once a month or once every other month – and share a Web link on something relevant to the line of work or corporate mission. If you come across a development that would interest that person, pass it along. You will want to walk the thin line between staying on the radar screen while not overloading the person, but *make the effort to stay connected.* Most other candidates will probably move on in their searches, but if and when something opens up and you've managed to maintain a promising connection with the interviewer, you've basically upped your chances of getting a phone call if and when something opens up at the firm or, if you're really lucky, at another she or he happens to know about. Plenty of people have gotten jobs not at firms where they applied but at others that interviewers recommended to them because they followed up and kept in touch. Your interviewer is connected to people outside his or her parent company, and making the necessary effort can pay off over time if you're patient enough and persistent enough to stay connected.

As a final point, consider this: Would you like to be job-searching for an entire year (yes, some job searches during difficult economic times can take this long if not longer), or would you rather stay in touch with an employer throughout that year and find out the following summer that there is finally an opening that fits you. In short, *playing the long game* can often help you reduce the time required for your search even if it appears to lengthen it at the outset.

Takeaway Points

- *Always remember that doing your homework means more than checking a Web site.* Learn as much as you can about a company before the interview. The more you know, the more you can set yourself apart from your competitors when it comes to interviewing.

- *Think in advance what questions to ask and what questions you can expect to be asked.* Most initial interview questions are similar, and with practice you should be able to come up with some prepared responses to help you present yourself in a convincing manner.

- *Practice your answers and watch your speed.* Rehearsals help you catch which phrases might convey inaccurate or dangerous meanings while also giving you time to measure your pace. You obviously don't want to recite your responses mechanically, but aim for enough practice so that your words come smoothly and comfortably.

- *Do a dry run before the interview.* Even a quick drive to and from the location the night before can help you avoid wrong turns or parking problems on the big day. Leave as little as possible to chance.

- *Note as much as you can about the conditions of the office.* Make mental notes of the people and setting. Ask yourself if this is a place where you can see yourself working.

- *Make notes after leaving the interview.* You will want to record any questions that stumped you or that you were not fully prepared for. Similarly, you'll want to note any issues that came up during the interview that give you pause about the position.

- *Follow up regardless of what happens.* Use your calendar programs to make reminders about when to send follow-up messages or letters. Reference specifics from the interview and reiterate how your background can match them.

- *Learn to deal with rejection, but don't let it stop you.* Part of any job search requires learning how to deal with being let down. If something really doesn't feel right or fair, step back and give it more thought; but don't let your pride stop you from following up anyway if you think there's a chance for something down the line. Remember, your interviewer could be a key to another job with a different firm or a connection to the company when something else opens up in six months. Make the effort to stay in touch.

DEALING WITH DISAPPOINTMENT

*Jonathan Cape was reportedly once asked by a woman
at a London cocktail party whether he kept copies
of his books. "Madam," he replied. "I keep thousands."*

U ndoubtedly, the most difficult part of any job search is quite simply dealing with the constant stream of rejections. Maybe you get a form email several weeks after not hearing back – maybe your name is even misspelled in the message two different times – or maybe you never heard any responses to any of your follow up messages. Maybe you got a call back about a second interview that somehow never materialized. Maybe after several promising discussions and promises of an offer everything goes…silent. You've done everything you know how to do up to this point and put in all this incredible effort, but after several weeks or months, all you have to show for it is heartbreak and frustration.

It's cliché and easy to say, "Expect this and learn to deal with it," but the fact is everyone gets discouraged during the job search. A common rule of thumb once had it that for every $10,000 a person made, he or she needed to expect to spend at least a month job searching for a similar position. In other words, if you wanted to make $50,000 a year, you had to expect to spend at least five months searching. Whether this is true (or ever was) is probably debatable, but nevertheless, a few notes bear mention:

- Statistics vary, but the average salesperson probably lands only one opportunity for every 10-20 outreaches or phone calls he makes. This means he has to call 20 people before he can expect to land not a sale but the *opportunity* for one. He also probably has to go through *four or five opportunities* to land a sale. Doing the math tells you that heartache outnumbers success by a factor of at least 100 to 1.

- The average direct-mail solicitation has a response rate of *three to five percent*. This means that for every 100 letters that a company mails out for a magazine subscription or purchase, they can only expect to hear back from between three and five potential customers.

The point is not that we all need to have the same drive and passion that salespeople have. Rather, we simply need to accept the fact that *job searches take time*. Sure, you may know of a number of friends who landed something shortly after college after having a couple of promising internships or whose parents had connections that helped them land an entry-level job. But people who start out of college with no such benefits or who lacked those kinds of assistance platforms have to build their networks from scratch, and that is something that is simply never done overnight. It requires an unbelievable amount of perseverance and commitment – the kind you probably would not have ordinarily in most any other respect – but that you will have to have in order to land your first job outside of college.

"Anyone who tells you they never gave up is probably full of it," said one job seeker. "I've given up more times than I can count after getting one too many rejections, but I always come back and keep searching, because in the end, it's all you can do. You can't quit, because there is no alternative."

Next Steps

If after a few weeks or months you still have not landed an interview or received an offer, step back and re-evaluate. Is your resume highlighting the kinds of successes you need to land the job you want? Does it fit the format that companies are expecting, or is it still following an outdated template that you got from a library book that is out of print? Does your online profile match the resumes you have been sending out to prospective employers on e-mail, or have you been remiss in updating one version or the other? Do you have too many versions of your resume in circulation to track?

The point is, *don't be afraid to experiment if nothing happens after a while.* If your old approach is not working, try something different. Was there a particular version of your resume that got more responses than others? If so, try and see what made that one stand out. Do you have friends who recently landed jobs? What did their resumes look like compared to yours, and what formats, templates, and fonts were they using? Did they highlight any skills sets that you've overlooked? Like any marketing and advertising campaign, you always need to be looking for what is reaching your target market; and that means making notes for what works and what does not.

Okay, you say, but suppose I've done *that* but still have nothing to show for it? Take a look at your network and your outreach efforts. Again, look at the successes you had or promising leads you developed that fizzled for one reason or another. Was there anything in common in any of them that you might have missed? Are most of your contacts people from your online social networks instead of the college alumni office or work groups? Have you been reaching out to professional groups in your area and going to events as often as other people in your network? See if you've been fishing too long in the same pond and need to branch out – ruts are easy to fall into, most of the time because we seldom realize we are in them until the frustration reaches a fever pitch.

What about your follow-ups? Have you been staying in steady contact with the people you meet and interview, or are you writing one or two e-mails and then forgetting about them? People want to be remembered. Make more notes on your calendar to follow up and see what you can be doing to help the people you reach out to. Does someone need something proofed by a second pair of eyes? Is there a blog someone is trying to launch but can't find the time to manage? Don't be afraid to divide your time by getting involved in some community projects or helping friends with some of their priorities – the change in pace may not only help you maintain a better mental balance, but it will also giving you something to take your mind off your search.

Reaching Back

Okay, suppose you've done everything you can and had several interviews, but something always seems to keep you from landing the golden prize. If you really want to show just how much *chutzpah* you've got, suck it up and make a list of the various places you've applied and been rejected from. Look it over and pick out the ones you really wanted or thought you had a promising shot of landing only to find yourself let down. Then, fire up your computer, take a deep breath, and get ready to shock some people.

You're going to ask for critical feedback.

That's right. *Ask them* if there was anything in your background or interview that came across in some way that inadvertently hurt your chances. You want to ask up front and professionally what might have made you come up short so you can address it in the future. No one improves from praise as much as from criticism, so don't be afraid of reaching back to see what some people might tell you. (Just be prepared to deal with the lack of response and negative response if and when any replies come back.)

A good possible method might be something like this:

To: Irene Interviewer

From: Janet Jobseeker

Hi, Irene –

I just wanted to say thanks again for taking some time a few weeks ago to interview me for the _____ position. I really enjoyed talking with you and learning more about ABC Company.

I also wanted to ask – honest! - if you could let me know whether there was anything in my background or our discussions that affected my prospects for the position. I know we all learn only if we get corrective feedback, so if there was something I could be doing in the future to help improve my

chances, I hope you'll let me know.

Again, many thanks. I hope all else is well and that we have a

chance to connect again.

Best,

Janet Jobseeker

For legal reasons, it is likely that most employers will refrain

from being too specific in any responses, assuming they send

them at all. Being too detailed in a rejection letter opens too

many risks that companies would prefer to avoid from a

liability standpoint; however, it's possible that Janet may still

receive one or two responses from earlier prospective

employers that give her some insight as to why she may have

been passed over.

This is not to suggest that such responses will be numerous or likely. In fact, it's highly likely that she will hear nothing at all or, at best, a generic response that alludes to the other candidate having more "specialized experience in areas that best suit our needs at this time." But just as with the 1 in 20 responses for the proverbial salesperson or 3 in 100 for a direct mail campaign, once in a while Janet may glean something that helps her in her search. She might even receive something like this:

To: Janet Jobseeker

From: Irene Interviewer

Hi, Janet -

Thanks for your e-mail. I can't think of anything – and for legal reasons, I obviously can't say much beyond what we discussed – but you may want to check back with us again after you've done more professional editing. Our supervisors usually look for people with 2-3 years of professional experience on top of the undergraduate work you mentioned in our discussion.

I'm sorry I can't be of more help. Best of luck in the job search!

Sincerely,

Irene Interviewer

While Janet's initial response to Irene's e-mail may well be to want to throw her laptop against the wall – she can't *get* any professional experience until someone hires her, and no one will apparently hire her without any professional experience –a closer look at what Irene wrote may give Janet some possible insight. The company wants people with professional experience in addition to undergraduate work. This means that Janet's resume, while impressive in terms of the work she listed for the school paper and campus magazine, probably lacked something in this regard that one of her counterparts had that tipped the scales in her favor.

Okay, so what is Janet to do? She can't possibly *get* any experience without being hired, so she is in the classic catch-22 every recent graduate faces. What are her options?

Actually, there are several. First, Janet should e-mail Irene back and thank her for following up and for being honest with her. (Remember, Irene could simply have deleted the message without responding, so while her feedback may indeed have been difficult to read, the fact that she took the time to give it should not be discounted.) Janet may have to type the e-mail through gritted teeth, but learning when to swallow one's pride goes with the job search.

Next, Janet should ask herself where she might begin getting some editing experience outside of school. Can she work with a volunteer organization and help with its online newsletter? Does her local library have an online magazine that it publishes regarding book clubs or a speaker series? Does the local parent-teacher organization have a newsletter that spells out what returning students should do in preparation for the new school year? Are there civic or community organizations that publish information about food drives and recycling programs? The point is that *somewhere* in Janet's neighborhood, there are likely several different groups or activist organizations that would benefit from her talents – even in a volunteer capacity – and while they might not necessarily be able to pay her for her work, helping them will give her some additional experience outside of her school listings. Bonus: It may help broaden her network of contacts as well.

Fine, you say. But suppose Janet is not looking for a volunteer position but instead for full-time work? Free assistance may be generous and nice, but it doesn't put food in the refrigerator or keep the lights on. True enough. But just as we all learn to crawl before we can walk and walk before we can run, so Janet needs to think longer term in relation to her job search. If she volunteers now, she gets some additional experience beyond school. If she gets that, she improves her professional credentials in the eyes of potential employers. If she does that, she improves her chances at landing a job. Painful as it is to recognize, the job search is a marathon, not a sprint. Spending some time volunteering now can pay benefits over the course of several months that the same time spent fruitlessly job searching might not.

Put another way, suppose Janet Jobseeker and Joe Jobsearcher are waiting tables at the same restaurant and looking to move into full-time salaried jobs. Janet reaches out to some of these groups to see where she can help them with their work while Joe Jobseeker does not. Janet quickly builds a small network of civic groups she helps by editing their flyers and proofreading blog postings while Joe focuses exclusively

on finding a paying editing position in the same town while

waiting tables. After six months, both of them are still

searching, but in the seventh month they both learn of an

opening across town. Which one has the better shot at landing

the position if both their undergraduate resumes show *exactly*

the same experiences in school? Joe has only his

undergraduate work going for him while Janet has at least a

few organizations that may be willing to speak on her behalf

and that she can provide samples from to give a prospective

employer an idea of what she can do.

The point is, by doing a little more outside of school –

even volunteering – Janet has improved her marketability.

Granted, the difference may be marginal in terms of actual

skills developed or abilities she's learned, but in the eyes of

prospective employers, she has already moved beyond the

work she did in school; Joe has not. (And Janet might not have gotten around to making this effort had she not reached out to Irene for the constructive feedback she got that put her on the path to getting the additional experience she would need to land that first job. This is why following up – even if the feedback sometimes makes for difficult digestion – is so critical. Without it, you can't learn where you may be falling short and address the issue.)

Remember, chances are few reach-back efforts will deliver anything too concrete, but don't let that keep you from trying. Think of it this way: A company may have something to lose by being too honest about why you were rejected (which is why it will always be a long shot to hear anything back), but since you have already been turned down, there is literally *nothing for you to lose by asking*. If you ask for some feedback and none is given, you are no worse off than had you never asked for the feedback in the first place. Swallow some pride and make the effort.

Next Networks

Another reason for staying in touch and reaching out to people even after a rejection – besides the fact that you may still have your sights set on the firm and can't take no for an answer just yet – is that those people may have connections at similar firms looking to hire people with comparable backgrounds. If you make a connection with that person, you open yourself up to his or her network and possibly develop the kind of connection that could lead to another job someplace else even if your first encounter with your primary contact came up short somehow.

Go back to Joe and Janet for a moment. Suppose they both interview for the same editing position, but Janet gets the job. Joe, realizing that he needs to make some changes in how he's approaching his search, makes an effort to stay in touch not just with Janet but also the recruiter they both spoke with. If that recruiter changes jobs and goes to work for another firm in a similar line of work, she may remember Joe and contact him in the event a similar position opens up at her new place of work.

Or perhaps the recruiter attends an HR networking meeting. Over the course of dinner and drinks, she learns of an opening at another company that would be a perfect fit for someone like Joe. Even better, the person who tells her of this opening is a person that the recruiter owes a favor or two. She might text Joe on the way home and tell him to reach out to her or pass his name along as a referral. Two weeks later, Joe could very well be sitting in another office interviewing for another job, only this time it's for one that has not been advertised yet and for which he is not competing against Janet. Consequently, even though he might have come up short against his former coworker, he may very well wind up looking spectacular when compared to the other people that this firm is considering.

The main point is, *you never know when a contact might lead to another opportunity.* Even if your initial connection is unfavorable or does not lead to an offer, there is always the potential for something else to develop down the line. Countless people have spent decades – if not entire careers – at places they never expected to be because one thing initially led to something that led to something else. Recognize that your potential connections can come from anyone, any time – and don't be afraid to look at rejections as setbacks rather than the end of the line. You never know who might come through for you.

Staying in Touch Afterward

Admittedly, this may seem like putting the cart before the horse in terms of timing, but assuming you're ultimately successful in landing a position, *make a point to stay in touch with the people you met during your job search.*

This is not as easy as it sounds. Once you've landed a job, the incentive to keep reaching out and staying connected dwindles while your plate is rapidly filled with other, more pressing priorities that require your attention. You won't have the same time as before to network, and you may find it takes days to get around to responding to e-mails compared to just moments when you were at home pounding away on the keyboard as you searched for that next lead. Nevertheless, make a concerted effort to maintain your network, even if it means having to put updates on your calendar to spend 20 or 30 minutes one night a week doing nothing but e-mailing old contacts just to stay in touch.

Common sense tells us that the reasoning behind this is simple, but ask anyone who has been in the workforce for years how often it happens. People may fall out of touch or lose contact; but the simple fact is that networking *never* stops being critical for job security and success.

Let's say you finally land that dream job. You spend a year learning the ropes and getting to know your dream profession. You get to travel, meet people, and build your resume. Then, one day – for no reason other than someone higher on the company totem pole thinks it will save the company money – your department is told to downsize. As one of the youngest people collecting an entry-level salary and with no tenure requiring an extended severance, you come in one day to find yourself told to report to HR. Within 20 minutes, you're told that your employment is terminated and that you need to clean out your desk. A representative from HR escorts you back to your cubicle where you pack your things, and moments later find yourself out on the street with no warning of what was coming or understanding of why you're now out of a job.

Sound brutal? Such stories happen every day in the corporate world; we just always think they happen to someone else. Now, ask yourself, which person is more likely to land on his feet: The person who has kept in touch with his original job search network and expanded it, or the person who gave up staying in touch with people after landing that all-important first job?

The days of people landing a job with one firm and spending their lives working their way up the corporate ladder until one day reaching the executive suite are long gone. True, we sometimes read about someone who manages to rise to the top after a long and successful career at a particular company, but such people are far more often the exception rather than the rule. If the average person can expect to work at half a dozen firms (if not more) over the course of a lifetime, networking is a survival skill everyone needs to learn and practice, even happy with a job.

But what if your present firm finds out about your attending a networking event or job fair? Well, admittedly attending such functions may not be the most politically savvy

things to share with your coworkers over coffee the next day,

but the truth is few if any employers can realistically expect

employees not to keep an eye out for better or stronger

opportunities in today's job market, particularly younger

workers fresh out of school. (Again, to every rule there is the

occasional exception, and while some firms or bosses may not

exactly smile on any networking activities if they are

discovered, bear in mind that any place that doesn't understand

why someone actively cultivates a network probably doesn't

have a firm grasp on the realities of the job market or has never

been downsized. In either case, their issues are not your

problem; you need to be watching out for what's best for *you*.)

Should you ever find yourself in the position of having to

explain why you were at a particular job event or networking

function, simple honesty and directness can go a long way:

"I've had too many friends who thought their jobs were safe

who wound up being let go unexpectedly, so I always make an effort to keep in touch with people in my field. It helps me stay current on the latest issues, and it sometimes even helps me learn about people who may benefit our company." This is all you need to say. Most if not all employers will respect this reasoning; and while it may be small comfort to learn unexpectedly that you work for one that does not, chances are any firms that don't respect this are not ones you want to spend a great deal of your future time working for in the first place.

What to Do

Do the same thing you did while searching for your job. Make notes on your calendar to drop someone a line every few weeks to make sure you don't lose touch. Forward the occasional link to something that you know from your discussions might interest that person. Don't worry if the interest is personal or professional, just make sure to maintain the connection over time. Dropping them a line once a week might be excessive, but few people mind getting an e-mail every two or three months from someone they look forward to hearing from. Your job is to find a way to be that someone so that if and when opportunities open up, you are there to take advantage of them.

And never forget, *networking is a two-way street.*

Takeaway Points

- *Always remember, <u>frustration goes with the job search</u>.* Telling yourself this is obviously easier than accepting it, but being overly optimistic and expecting a short transition can be just as harmful as beating yourself up over a search that takes several months. There is no "right" amount of time for job searching – what takes two equally skilled people can take vastly different amounts of time for no other reason than luck.

- *Never stop experimenting.* The only way to avoid a rut is to constantly see what else you can try that works and then noting whatever results in a promising response. Make a point from time to time in your search to look back at what you've been trying and see what else might work.

- *Don't be afraid to reach back for feedback.* You never know what might be tipping the scales against you unless someone tells you. Maybe something as simple as your choice of white socks with a dress suit or the multiple ear piercings you have caught your interviewer's attention in something other than a positive way. Not asking means never knowing.

- *Never stop networking.* Your rejector could be your future acceptor if circumstances change; or someone who passes on you as an employee might know of someone else who would still be interested in what you have to offer. Make a point to stay in touch, and never let the acceptance of a job keep you from maintaining your contact with the people in your network – remember, a constant communicator will always have the edge over someone who drops out of sight after landing a job.

YOU'RE HIRED! (*NOW* WHAT???)

*"Failure...is difficult to bear, but very few
can manage the shock of early success."*

- *Maurice Valency*

Nothing lasts forever, the saying goes, and neither does your job search (although it will certainly feel like forever during the process). Eventually, through trial, error, and sheer perseverance, you will ultimately land a job that catapults you from the world of waiting tables and punching cash registers to an office life. Some of your experiences will be just as you imagined (petty issues that get blown out of proportion, personality squabbles, etc.), some will be painful (illegal and unethical behavior, seamy backstabbing, etc.), and some of it will be beyond your imagination ("People really behave this way?!?!"). Through it all, however, your goal should remain the same: *to get as much from the job as you can learn before moving on to something else.*

Depending on the firm, industry, and your own fortune (or – occasionally – a lack of it), you will sooner or later move up or move on when the time comes. This chapter is about making sure you plant your feet firmly after landing and how to make sure things go as smoothly as possible during your time in the job, whether it's several years or only a few months.

You're Hired, *Now* What?

Once you receive the offer letter confirming the details of your position – your title, start date, agreed salary, and so forth – then and only then should you give notice to your current employer. Yes, this applies even if that job involves bagging groceries at the supermarket or parking cars. Regardless of how anxious you are to leave a bad job or are looking forward to starting a new one, and as the saying goes, verbal offers are seldom if ever worth the paper they are printed on. *Never give notice without a written offer.*

Sound obvious? It's not. "I once accepted a verbal offer that was later rescinded," one job seeker said. "The company made me the offer and told me everything was all set, so I went into work the next day and gave my notice. When I got back to my desk, I saw my message light blinking and thought, 'Oh, no. That's not good.' It turned out I was right; the supervisor who wanted to hire me was told by *his* supervisor that for budget reasons they needed to put the position on hold. He tried to tell his boss that he'd already made the offer and it had been accepted, but his boss said no way. They had to take back the offer, and I had to go down to

HR and withdraw my notice." She paused. "Not only was that not a good day for me, but I'd tipped my hand at the company I was working for that I was unhappy and thinking about leaving. Things were never the same afterward." The company that initially made her the offer later added insult to injury by telling the prospective employee that they would not be filling her position after all. "I learned after that to always, *always* get offers in writing before giving notice," she adds.

But let's assume that you've been given the offer and that everything matches up with what you've been expecting. You've done your homework on the company, and your sources all tell you it's a good place to work. How do you go about making the transition from new hire to employee?

Onboarding

Most companies, particularly large firms, have a standard process known as *onboarding*. Like the name sounds, this is the process by which a new employee "comes onboard" and gets introduced to the company, its policies and goals, and how it operates. These will usually be conducted during your first few weeks on the job. Here are a few things you can expect:

- **You will need to bring some proof of identification.** Most companies require two types of identification to verify you are in fact who you say you are. Documents can include a driver's license, valid passport, and/or a birth certificate. Employees on work visas or who are non-native workers will be required to bring additional paperwork. Plan on bringing some identification with you during your first few days; you probably won't need to present it after your first day, but bring it along during your first week in case there are any slip-ups with paperwork or processing and keep them handy in a folder at home. Filling out the same paperwork repeatedly because of slip-ups in HR happens more frequently than you might think.

- **Find out what you will be expected to wear.**
  While many organizations have long since gone "business casual," remember that what constitutes "casual" at one may not necessarily be acceptable in another. Put another way, what passes for casual at a dot-com vs. a very conservative brokerage firm or financial planning office are likely to be two separate extremes – jeans and t-shirts may be fine at the former but seldom at the latter. When in doubt, err on the side of caution rather than on risk. You don't want your first day to be one where you inadvertently get off on the wrong footing by failing to measure up to an expected standard someone

never mentioned to you but which you never inquired about, either.

- **Expect to talk and sign a lot of paperwork.** Your first few hours will likely be spent in HR going over paperwork and legal requirements. There will probably be required sessions you have to sit through regarding company policy, procedures, and likely disciplinary measures for any infractions. You will likely have to sign a lot of documents verifying your receipt of materials, such as employee handbooks or computers and software; however, you will also be required to sign a lot of other documents as well, such as nondisclosure agreements in the event you will be given access to proprietary information, anti-sexual harassment documents verifying that you have read and understood company policies regarding inappropriate behavior, tax and withholding forms, direct deposit banking forms, and others. Expect your writing hand to get a workout.

- **Expect to talk with a lot of people during your first few days on the job.** Again, this more likely applies when the company is a large firm vs. a smaller one or start-up operation; however, you can and should expect to meet and talk with a lot of people throughout the organization. Many of these will include people in your department and work area, but also those in other departments, like payroll, supplies, computer systems, HR, and others. Bring a notebook and take as many notes as possible, particularly of any people you meet and talk with and what their role in the organization happens to be. You will want to refer to these later when you need to know who handles which operation in the company. Remember, networking requires internal as well as external efforts.

- **Look for a "buddy."** This person is your assigned go-to individual for any questions you have during your first few weeks on the job. Some companies assign these, others expect you to find one for yourself. He or she will be the one who helps get you acquainted with the people you need to know, as well as where you can go for further information. Try not to overload the buddy with too many questions initially – you'll find you learn a lot just by observing and keeping your ears open – but don't be afraid to reach out for help when something comes up that you don't understand. A good method to employ is to keep a list handy of any questions you need answered as they come up and then to meet with your buddy at a pre-arranged time to go over them. This helps give the other person time to manage his or her daily needs in addition to yours while also setting up an agreed time where he or she will be fresh and able to focus on giving you full attention to answer questions. It also looks far more professional than popping by your buddy's desk each time something comes up requiring his/her input and attention.

- **Treat the people you meet like your network contacts.** Take some time during these first critical days and weeks to get to know them, their likes and dislikes, hobbies, work preferences, personality styles, and so forth. People usually love to talk about themselves, so a few small-talk questions aimed at getting to know them as people vs. just co-workers can go a long way toward laying a smooth foundation for a strong working relationship. Don't be afraid to ask about lunch plans or

recommendations on good local places to eat or

simply to grab a cup of coffee. Chances are that

any places they recommend will be spots other

people in the office frequent as well and that you'll

want to get to know as you familiarize yourself with

the neighborhood layout. Make some notes and try

to remember different things about each person –

don't worry. It will take time, but the payoff for

you in the long run will make it worthwhile.

At the end of your first few days, you will probably have

meetings scheduled with your boss to help get up to speed on

any pending projects that you will be expected to help with or

any planned initiatives the company will be looking to you to

help with. Think of these as lecture hall sessions where you

get a chance to learn and make notes for future reference.

Then, just as in school, take the notes home in the evening and review them, making sure to understand what will be expected of you and noting what kinds of questions you have based on what you're told. Having them in a list format will help you to look organized and thoughtful vs. someone who simply asks questions or never follows up after a talk.

What if the Company Doesn't Have an Onboarding Plan?

Small firms, start-ups, mom-and-pop outfits, and other companies don't always have onboarding plans and processes. In these cases, you will have to make more of an effort to get to know the people you will be working with and learn what will be expected in terms of your performance.

If the company is a large firm that has only a minimal onboarding process, such as a Web overview of the corporate structure or pre-recorded outline of company history and policy that you are required to listen to and then sign an acknowledgment without an opportunity to ask questions, take it as a sign that your acclimation process is going to involve a lot of uphill climbing. Studies have repeatedly shown that companies that put a greater effort into helping new employees adjust to their jobs and surroundings suffer less turnover and frustration than those that do not. This is not to suggest that they are bad places to work, but your first few months are likely to be more difficult without a more defined process compared to other companies with such procedures.

Fine, you say. That's all well and good, but how does knowing that help me? What if I was told about an onboarding process but find I need more information or that the instruction I've been given doesn't tell me all I need to know? This is when you will need to develop your own list of onboarding priorities to help you get up to speed. Think about what you will need to know to hit the ground running and aim to become as familiar as possible with what you'll need to know as quickly as you can. A good way to do this is to put together your own sample onboarding outline and go through it with your boss. (See Fig. 1.)

Figure 1
Personal Development Plan

Name: _____

Department: _____

Supervisor: _____

Start Date: _____

Week 1

- ❑ Complete HR paperwork and registration process; attend any new-employee orientations, seminars, and activities
- ❑ Meet with supervisor to discuss goals, performance expectations, etc.
- ❑ Get introduced to coworkers in unit
- ❑ Learn location of office basics (restroom, kitchen, copier, mail room, etc.)
- ❑ Begin developing basic understanding of office work procedures
- ❑ Begin meeting with key personnel in company (accounting/payroll, IT, HR, etc.) to understand who the "go to" people are for issues
- ❑ Begin meeting with representatives from other departments to understand their roles in organization, who the key contacts are, etc.
- ❑ Schedule end-of-week meeting with supervisor to go over events of week
- ❑ Make a point of going to coffee or lunch with at least one new coworker
- ❑ Other: _____

Week 2

- ❑ Meet with supervisor to discuss goals, performance expectations, etc.
- ❑ Determine which key people in company still to be met, what their roles in the company are, and how your job affects what they do and vice versa
- ❑ Attend any follow-up activities and seminars
- ❑ Work out "shadowing" arrangements with people in office to learn what they do and how they do it (sit in on sales calls, act as "silent observer" for meetings and teleconferences, etc.)
- ❑ Identify areas of possible contribution (where you can make a difference, assist with a project, or provide input, etc.)
- ❑ Make a point of going to lunch or coffee with at least one new coworker
- ❑ Other:

Week 3

- ❑ Meet with supervisor to finalize expectations, establish preliminary goals, and outline preferred communication style (weekly updates vs. monthly)
- ❑ Identify any remaining people in office you need to meet and get to know (particularly if any have been out of the office or on vacation during the previous weeks)
- ❑ Continue "shadowing" people in different departments to continue broadening your knowledge and understanding
- ❑ Other:

This is admittedly just a basic outline of some possible initial activities you can envision, but these steps and others are commonly found in most office orientation and new employee programs. The goal is to get you well acquainted with as many people in the office as possible so that you quickly develop relationships that enable to you to not only feel "at home" but which also help you to grow and learn about the company and your role within it. People who do not develop such relationships or who simply come in, go to their desks, and then leave automatically at the end of the day may accomplish any number of things – some may even excel in research environments or lab studies – but for the most part, absent any attachment or ability to relate to those around them, such people invariably fail to develop a sense of cohesion or dedication to their jobs, and their performance is nearly always below what it could otherwise be if they had a stronger connection to their coworkers and the organization overall.

Okay, you may be thinking, but suppose I'm a shy person? What if I'm the type who is most comfortable at the desk crunching numbers, proofing copy, or coming up with a graphic design concept in total solitude? Suppose I'm the kind who needs to shut things out in order to concentrate and perform at my best? What about folks with *my* personality and perspective? What do *we* do?

First, take a deep breath. During these first critical weeks on the job, you're going to need to push yourself in some ways that might not fit within your normal comfort zone. This means that even if you're a shy person or someone whose throat dries up at the very thought of talking to any number of people that exceeds one, you're going to have to find a way to overcome this reluctance, at least initially. Think of this as just another part of your job interview process – you were able to prepare for that, weren't you? Have a "script" of simple conversational questions to ask when you begin meeting your new coworkers. If necessary, try acknowledging your shyness and turning it into something for conversation. "In my last job, we didn't get around to knowing each other that well, but I really want to get to know people in this company, because I haven't made any plans for lunch and need to know a good place to eat nearby. Do you know of one?" Food is an excellent way of breaking down some interpersonal barriers. Perhaps you need to get a greeting card for someone on the way home that evening – no one needs to know if you do or don't in reality – but ask if there's a gift shop in the area or a supermarket where you can pick one up. Is there a coffee shop or bagel bakery nearby if you need a caffeine fix? What about the closest ATM machine or bank outlet? Is the dry cleaner down the street one people would recommend or one that can't be trusted not to damage people's clothes? Any number of these questions and items can serve as a good starting point for a brief conversation that can help you get past your initial shyness and help lay a foundation for building some bridges. The bottom line is, there are probably countless things you need to know about your new office and surroundings, and your first few weeks are the best time to start finding out about them. Use this time to your advantage.

Getting the Most from the Job

Far too many people spend far too much time at jobs they hate. They may feel that they are too old to look for another position, they may not feel that they will be able to command a comparable salary elsewhere, or they may simply be trying to "ride out" the working life until retirement when they can split for Florida. Such people are almost always negative, argumentative, and an energy drain on those around them.

You don't want to wind up as one of these people.

To guard against this, remember a rule of thumb as you go through your working career: *Am I still learning at this job, and is there more that it can teach me?* Bear in mind even CEOs who have held the top spot for a number of years describe their jobs as never-ending learning processes. Maybe they're learning new ways to deal with challenging members of the company Board of Directors or discovering new things about their competitors. Maybe there's a new direction they want the firm to pursue, and now they need to know the best way to get there. There is always something new to be learned.

Fine, you say, but how long is the right amount of time to hold a particular job? Generally, it's considered preferable to hold on to a job for a minimum of one year before switching; however, this has begun to change in today's fast-paced job world. That said, having two or three positions in a year is not something that is going to earn too many smiles upon a resume review. Plan to remain for a while unless something disastrous happens or a stunning offer lands in your lap. (Again, this is more a marathon than sprint.)

However, if after the first twelve or eighteen months at your first entry-level job you find yourself thinking, *"That's it?"* it may be time to think about whether to move up or move on. If there isn't a promotion on the horizon, better pay waiting, or if the job can't serve as a stepping stone to something more rewarding, it's probably not something you want to have for very long. Aside from the lack of interest or challenge, you also need to think about your competitive standing in the job market – spending five or six years at a comfortable or "cushy" job may mean low stress and a steady paycheck that helps you get by and pay the necessary bills, but when you do eventually decide to move on, you'll likely be competing against people who have had stronger track records (increased responsibilities, pay raises, promotions, etc.) at their jobs and who, more likely than not, are likely to be the kinds of candidates other firms are looking to hire when trying to bring someone on board. This won't necessarily be a major issue during your first few years out of school, but over time you will need to be able to demonstrate a strong track record of increased responsibility and achievement if you want to remain competitive and have a good shot at landing a future job with better pay and benefits.

Knowing When It's Time to Leave

Chances are you will know this on your own, but once you do start looking, make an effort not to draw attention to the fact. Rightly or wrongly, perception is reality; and if someone senses you might be short for the company, it won't be long before you find yourself marginalized or worse.

"I made the mistake of letting my employer know I was going for my MBA at a part-time program," said one employee. "I had planned eventually to leave the firm since there weren't any promotional opportunities available, but I wanted to be professional about it. Unfortunately, once the word got out, people began perceiving me as a 'short timer' and I was left out of meetings and discussions that involved a number of the projects I was working on. After one particularly stressful incident, I went into a conference room with my supervisor to have it out; and the first thing she asked me was, 'Why are you still here? I thought you'd be gone by now.' That told me I not only had no future at the firm, but my present was done as well."

When you do begin looking around for another job, expect finding the time to interview to be difficult. Most firms will probably understand and be agreeable to interviewing you after normal working hours, but don't be surprised if some do not. Like you, most people don't relish staying late in the office for any reason, particularly if they have families to go home to or personal commitments that require attention. Nevertheless, don't be afraid to ask if you can interview during early morning or late afternoon so as to minimize the "signal" you would otherwise be sending by taking time off in the middle of the day. Lunch time interviews are another possibility, but more often than not an hour will not be sufficient time to get to and from another office while still having enough time to meet with people and review your qualifications. (Remember, just because the interview may take an hour doesn't mean the overall interview experience itself will.)

Dressing for your interview will pose another challenge. If you have a connection or friend at the prospective employer – you may be able to bring a change of clothes by in the early morning to change into later – but otherwise you may have to weigh the risks of going to the interview in casual attire from your office vs. dressing up and tipping your hand.

On a related note, third or fourth interviews should usually be considered warning signs. While many firms may require screening tests and personality evaluations to ensure that you are a proper "fit" for the organization, once you are

brought in for face-to-face discussions, things should move

rapidly one way or another. If you're told after the second

interview that the company expects to make a decision shortly

but find yourself called back unexpectedly for a third, then

fourth, then *fifth* interview, a yellow warning light should be

going off, because this indicates some confusion or

miscommunication on the firm's part (i.e., telling you one thing

and then another later). You should certainly feel free to go if

the job sounds like a good match, but if the company decides

that a fourth or fifth round of interviewing is necessary before a

decision can be made, you should probably consider this a

major warning sign. Not only is the company not showing

respect your time – remember, you probably need to arrange

for time off from work each time for a face-to-face interview,

something that becomes increasingly difficult each time you

have to come up with an excuse for being out during the

middle of the day – but more than three interviews is usually a clear sign of managerial indecision on some level. Maybe there is a squabble between two managers over which responsibilities will "shift" over to the new hire once he or she is on board, or maybe the company can't make up its mind between you and another finalist. More likely than not, there are several layers of approval at the new firm, and someone at the top holds all the power of yes or no. Tell the interviewer that you appreciated the opportunity to meet with them but that you cannot schedule more time out of the office during normal business hours without sending a pretty clear signal that you are searching for another job. If they cannot make a decision after three – or at worst, four – face-to-face conversations, you are probably better off working someplace else.

Remember, you want a *good* job, not *any* job.

Leaving on a Positive Note

Okay, let's assume you've finally been extended an offer and accepted. Congratulations. Now, how exactly do you go about planning your exit?

YouTube™ videos and comedy routines to the contrary, it's generally never a good idea to burn a bridge, particularly when you are just starting out in the working world. Professional networks are surprisingly broad in terms of their reach, so you need to make an effort not to leave on bad terms. If you are pressed upon giving your resignation for reasons, be honest but don't rehash issues regarding your present job or problems you have had with coworkers. Tell your supervisor that the other firm made an offer with more growth opportunities or a higher salary offering and that your decision was simply business. Above all, *never let anyone make you feel guilty about leaving a job.* Supervisors who attempt to lay a guilt trip or appeal to you on personal levels do you no favors. If you're leaving during a difficult or busy time, expect some expressions of regret or frustration, but stick to your guns and keep your tone businesslike and professional. The bottom line – and there is simply no getting around it – is this: it's not about your employer's interests now but *what's best for you.*

Sound selfish? Welcome to the working world. For good or bad, right or wrong, these are the issues that every job seeker (and every employer) weighs when making a hiring decision. (Really want to be mercenary? Ask yourself if the company would sweat cutting *you* if it made business sense and reduced overhead. It would be a business decision and not personal, right? Same goes for you.) Nevertheless, it's still a better strategy to try and part on as good a set of terms as possible. A good strategy for this is to help lay some ground work for your successor. Take some time and review the onboarding information you compiled or that the company put you through and think about what might be essential for the new employee to know when she or he joins the firm that is not covered during orientation and onboarding sessions. Maybe there are some tricks you know that will make the job easier that you can job down for some handy reference notes. If you still have a copy of your original job description, go over it and make some polite suggestions to your boss about any ways it might be updated or changed to reflect the way your job is currently structured vs. the way it was when you first started. If you really want to go above and beyond, leave some contact info where you can be reached in the event anyone has any questions about files or procedures. You should be willing to help out during the first few weeks while at your new job, but be firm in telling the people at your old job that you are starting a new position with another company and that their needs are going to be foremost on your mind during your first few days and weeks there as you lay the groundwork for more success there. If you continue getting calls and e-mails asking for more information, delay replying until the evening. Replying after hours should send the signal that it's time for the company to move on and let you start doing your new job. If the efforts persist and become disruptive – if your old boss keeps calling you at your new job with questions or problems – recognize that while you don't want to burn a bridge, you also don't want to damage the one you're trying to build at your new office either, particularly during the first critical weeks and months. Set a time frame after which you will no longer be able to provide assistance. If calls and questions continue after a couple of months, tell your old firm that you're either no longer available or that you will be happy to help *for a modest consulting fee*. Chances are the calls and messages will cease immediately.

The Exit Interview

For legal and business purposes, most companies require a 20- or 30-minute exit interview of all their employees. Basic issues will be covered – have you turned over any sets of keys to filing cabinets that you have, returned any software or computer materials, etc. – but you will also likely be asked a number of questions about your time with the firm, the people you worked with, and so forth.

Be very careful which words you use to discuss any difficulties you might have had while working at the firm. While you don't necessarily want to be dishonest regarding any particular issues, you also don't want to use the exit interview as the sort of full-steam venting session that's better suited for a therapist's office than your HR department. Chances are anything you say – regardless of its veracity – will simply be noted in a file and then forgotten, so expecting or hoping that your constructive criticism will lead to changes is more often than not wishful thinking. You may have been treated unfairly by your boss or some coworkers, but unless their behavior crosses serious ethical or legal lines – and even if it does – the greater likelihood is that the behavior will be noted but little action taken. (If you are sexually harassed or suffered racial taunts or something similar, you may obviously want to note these in your exit interview. But more often than not, however, people will try to forget unpleasant experiences by departing employees if for no other reason than because it is simpler to do so than to confront a problem head-on.) If there were some things you felt crossed a line, prioritize the ones you feel are most important and think about what you want to say, but leave the rest of your baggage out of the office. There's no point in jeopardizing a graceful exit by appearing petty or unhappy about something that is unlikely to be changed after you leave.

As we said, *it's just business.*

Takeaway Points

- *Expect your first days to be critical but not intimidating.* Make an effort to get to know your new coworkers and the procedures you will be expected to follow. If the company you're joining does not have a formal onboarding plan, make an appointment to discuss a personalized one with your supervisor. It's his or her job to help you get your feet firmly planted and guide your growth with the firm.

- *Don't be shy.* Even if it's more in keeping with your personality to be quiet as opposed to loud, use the first few days at a new job as a chance to come out of your shell, even if for only a little while. Make an effort to get to know as many people as possible, both personally and professionally.

- *A job that no longer has something to teach you is not a job you should have any longer.* If you've already mastered all the responsibilities for your position, it's time to think about moving up or – if necessary – moving on. It's perfectly acceptable to have a comfort zone; but don't let it become a bubble that you're afraid to pop because you fear change. Few people in their twilight years look back on their lives with satisfaction over not having taken many risks. More often than not, it's the opposite that they regret.

- *Make as positive an exit as possible.* Swallow some pride if you have to, but make your best effort to leave on a high note. Trashing coworkers or venting about issues you felt were grossly unfair usually only serves to make you look petty and disagreeable. If you must raise serious ethical or professional wrongdoings, plan ahead how you will discuss them and make sure to prioritize which are worth mentioning and which – no matter how frustrating – can be let go.

THOUGHTS TO KEEP IN MIND

*"I think I did pretty well, considering I started
out with nothing but blank paper."*

- *Steve Martin*

B en Franklin was once said to have commented, "The only thing we learn about common sense is that it isn't." Many of the tips and strategies outlined in this book may seem trivial or obvious at first glance, but a quick talk with any hiring manager or business professional will quickly reveal how few people really understand the importance of careful networking and follow-through.

If you take away only a few things from reading this, remember that *connections are everything.* Want to know why so many people get their hair cut and start dressing professionally once they leave college? Because they can no longer afford to leave anything to chance when it comes to making a strong impression and establishing a connection with someone. Sure, show business has its share of rebels, and sports figures will always earn millions for seeming defiant and claiming not to care what people think; but never forget that, more often than not, everything these people wear, do, and say is often marketed or cleared with a PR agent or manager. The image presents a financial benefit, and it's one that never reflects what truly goes on once the cameras are turned off. (Want to see how quickly things change for a rock star or actor? Watch the video when they appear before a judge after their latest PR stunt or arrest; even the most outlandish rebel will wear something respectful and show deference to the judge.)

If you're a working stiff – i.e., the other 99 percent of the population – you don't have the luxury of being a professional provocateur. Sure, some people earn large paychecks for courting controversy and publicity, but unless you're one of them and earning millions in royalties or a fat book contract, you must always be conscious of the message and image you project. Rightly or wrongly, for the rest of your professional life you will depend one way or another on the people you meet every day. These may be new contacts at a company you're hoping to work for someday, or they may include the barista at the local coffee shop who – it just so happens – turns out to have a friend who works at a local design firm who would be happy to pass your resume along if you e-mail it to him/her. The point here is, *you can never know who will ultimately be that next connection.* Sometimes a person you barely know may bend over backwards to help you;

conversely, someone you thought was a close friend but who

lucked out and landed a job right out of school and who doesn't

understand the difficulty of a long job search may not be able

to offer more than help with the happy hour tab. The point is,

people will always surprise you, in both good and bad ways,

while others – sometimes the ones that you least expect – will

come through for you and go to bat for you time and again.

But since you never know, *leave as little as possible to chance.*

Why? Because more often than not, those people who

are most willing to lend a hand or provide a referral have at one

time or another themselves been put down, laid off, or suffered

some other indignity. Unlike people who fell into careers right

away after college or whose families were able to hook them

up with cushy paying gigs, these people know or remember all

too well how difficult it can be to get a leg up on finding a new

job. Someone, somewhere, gave them a lucky break that

helped them get their start, and your job – your job before *getting a job* – is to make sure you're always prepared and ready for that one break when it arrives.

Put another way, opportunity does not knock very often; so it will be up to you to always be ready when it comes time to answer the door.

Takeaway Points

Never, ever, leave anything to chance if you can possibly help it. Chance invites uncertainty and error; and the more you can do to reduce it – you can never entirely eliminate it – the stronger your chances for landing a particular job. Wondering how long it takes to get somewhere for an interview? Do a dry run. Have the name of the person you're going to be meeting with? Look them up on social media and job networking sites to see what you can learn about them. The more you know, the better your chances.

Never pass up a chance to make a connection. A well-known anecdote tells the story of a farmer who showed up at an expensive dealership to buy a car for his daughter upon her graduation. The farmer was in his overalls and smelled of earth and manure, and – not surprisingly – none of the fancy salespeople were interested in helping him. After all, it wasn't as if he gave the appearance of being able to afford anything on the lot anyway! (The farmer might have benefited from some of the suggestions in this book about not leaving things to chance, but that's a different story.)

Finally, one of the salespeople went over to the farmer and began to talk with him. When the farmer introduced himself, the salesperson recognized his name instantly. The farmer was the *largest landowner in the state* and one of the wealthiest citizens as well. He bought a car from that salesperson that day, but that was not all. Because he had shown the man courtesy when no one else did, the farmer made a point of buying *only from that salesman* for the rest of his life. For a few minutes of courtesy, the salesman got an eternal customer.

Another anecdote tells the story of a young entrepreneur who wanted to start his own lawn-care service. He saved his money and bought some equipment and a good power-mower, but he needed to find customers and learn how to grow his business. So, he went to a local businessmen's roundtable to see what he could learn. Once again, most of those in attendance could not be bothered with the young man. He obviously had no experience or relations with the other businessmen, and so he was ignored. Finally, one of the older men who owned a large company lamented that he wanted to do business with another company but could not think of a way to connect with its owner.

The young man's eyes lit up. "I can put you in touch with him," he said.

The older businessman looked back at him in disbelief. "How do *you* know him?" he asked.

"Simple," the young man answered. "I cut his lawn once a week."

Never stop networking.

INDEX

ABOUT THE AUTHOR

 John Franklin, CAPM, MBA is a writer and speaker who has spent more than 20 years working with job applicants to increase their networking and communication skills. His articles have appeared in several publications, including the Montgomery County *Business Record*, Prince William *Journal-Messenger*, *Amstat News*, *Education Update*, and the *Fairfax Connection*. He has appeared on the *PBS News Hour with Paul Solman* and spoken before audiences in the United States, Australia, Great Britain, Norway, and Sweden. He is the co-author and editor of *Priorities in Practice: World Languages* and lectures regularly on the importance of writing, editing, and public speaking. He is currently an instructor at the George P. Schultz National Foreign Affairs Training Center. He currently lives in Fairfax County, Virginia, with his wife Linda and their German shepherd, Sam.